Knitter's *Magazine Books*

Ethnic Socks & Stockings

A compendium of Eastern design & technique

Priscilla A. Gibson-Roberts

Photographed by Alexis Yiórgos Xenakis

SIOUX FALLS, SOUTH DAKOTA

Edited by Elaine Rowley

Ethnic **Socks &** **Stockings**

A compendium of Eastern design & technique

A Knitter's Magazine Book

EDITOR Elaine Rowley

PHOTOGRAPHERS
Alexis Yiórgos Xenakis
J. VanSant Roberts, B&W

CONSULTING EDITOR
Dorothy T. Ratigan

GRAPHIC DESIGNER
Mark Sampson

DIGITAL CONSULTANT
David Xenakis

PRODUCTION
Carol Skallerud CHIEF
Jay Reeve
Susan May
Lynda Selle
John Ashlock

The publishers would like to thank the following people and museums for their invaluable contribution: The Metropolitan Museum of Art, New York, New York #27.170.95 and #27.170.96 (ALL RIGHTS RESERVED, THE METROPOLITAN MUSEUM OF ART) MAMLUK 1; Lubenova Stancheva, Panaguriste, Bulgaria STRIPED BULGARIAN 2, BANDED BULGARIAN 20, 21, BULGARIAN MOTIF 24; Therese Inverso, Camden, New Jersey BAKHTIARI 3; Constance LeLena, Grand Junction, Colorado LUR 4; Arianthe Stettner, Steamboat Springs, Colorado NORTHEASTERN IRANIAN/AFGHANI 5; Frances Avery Oldsborg, Antrim, New Hampshire TURKISH 6; Peg Laflam, Franklin, New Hampshire IRANIAN SHEPHERD 7; Rae Erdahl, Madison, Wisconsin NATURAL TURKISH 8; Kathleen Rippberger, Carlsbad, California IRANIAN 9, CHILD'S 25; Olena Morozewych, Lakewood, Colorado UKRAINIAN 10; HELEN LOUISE ALLEN TEXTILE COLLECTION, SCHOOL OF FAMILY RESOURCES AND CONSUMER SCIENCES, University of Wisconsin-Madison, IRAQI 11, HENNAED 14; Miriam Milgram, New York, New York ALBANIAN 12, MACEDONIAN 18, BULGARIAN POINT PATTERN 19, SARAKATSANI 23; Gail Goss, Yakima, Washington BLACK SEA 13; Betty Avery, Antrim, New Hampshire EASTERN ANATOLIAN 15; Textile Collections, WITTE MUSEUM, San Antonio, Texas GEORGIAN 16; Nelda Davis, Milltown, New Jersey VERTICALLY PATTERNED TURKISH 17; Sara Hazelwood, Cedarburg, Wisconsin TUFTED TOE 22; Jeanne Hansen, Auburn, California BULGARIAN FLORAL MOTIF 26; Yusuf Nidai, Murat Kanli, and Seugul Siper, THE ACADEMY OF TURKISH MUSIC AND FINE ARTS, Sydney, Australia. We are greatly indebted to them.

Author's Acknowledgement: I cannot begin to thank all those involved in putting this book together. First, there were those who generously donated their socks to the project. There were those who willingly loaned their prized stockings, collected while traveling or working abroad or received as gifts from loved ones abroad. Often, these loans were for extended periods as I agonized over reproducing some specific technique. There were those who gave me leads to locating a choice sample or collection. There were those who willingly shared information, on occasion remembering some small detail that proved to be the clue in solving a knitting puzzle. There were those who provided direct assistance in the tedious process of recording designs, stitch by stitch, on graph paper. And others who assisted with housing and transportation, enabling me to see collections while traveling for workshops.

But most of all, I want to thank those who encouraged me to continue when I felt the project had overwhelmed my capabilities, badgered me when I was tired of the process and wanted to walk away, or, more importantly, just believed in me. In this latter category, I must single out four for special kudos. First, my friends: Nelda Davis, always there, always willing, regardless of what needed to be done; Kate Martinson, always supportive even though overwhelmed with her own responsibilities; Noel Thurner, always positive and upbeat, keeping life in perspective—all from half a continent away. And finally, my husband Jack—first for taking countless black and white photographs, but more so for believing that I had something special to say, even though the whole process was often an inconvenience. To my understanding editor Elaine Rowley, to my untiring manuscript reader Lizbeth Upitis, and all the other unnamed soulmates who assisted in countless ways, I extend my undying gratitude. As in past research efforts, I could not, would not, have stayed the course alone.

First published in USA in 1995 by XRX, Inc.
PO Box 1525, Sioux Falls, SD 57101-1525

Copyright © XRX, Inc. 1995

Library of Congress
Catalog Card Number: 95-60657

ISBN 0-9646391-0-6

Produced in Sioux Falls, South Dakota by XRX, Inc., 605-338-2450

Color separations by House of Graphics, South Sioux City, NE

Printed in Singapore

Contents

Ethnic socks are often glimpsed on festive occasions as part of a moving display of colorful costumes.
A few can be seen in museums, but they are rarely the focal point of the display.
In both cases, just enough is seen to catch the eye. For a real appreciation, a closer look is necessary:
top band of the Ukrainian sock (p. 34), BACKGROUND; Turkish wedding socks (pp. 30-31), HIS SOCKS.

Introduction

What began as a closer look at some wonderful socks grew into a study of a different knitting tradition. Priscilla A. Gibson-Roberts' mental unravelings of socks provide us with the excitement that comes from discovering a new approach to something as familiar as an old sock.

The immediate and obvious interest here is the wonderful patterning. Eastern knitters mix many colors and designs into stunning pieces of footwear. Twenty-six pairs are described and charted in Chapter 2 (p. 15).

The techniques used are as fresh and varied as the patterning. These socks almost all begin at the toe; most Western socks begin at the top. This single difference affects almost everything in between — from the way the stitches are cast on at the toe, to how (and when) the heel is worked, to the choice of finish at the top.

This book gives each reader a close look at these wonderful pieces of knitting. In *Historical Roots* (p. 9), we are reminded that the socks come from an area where even knit stitches were formed in a way unfamiliar to most of us.

After a look at the socks, *Construction Techniques* (p. 63) and *Design Techniques* (p. 81) are explained and illustrated. Try them out in the seven sampler socks, *Samplers* (p. 91). *East Meets West* (p. 101) gives general advice and a basic pattern for socks constructed in the Eastern way, but with a Western fit. A brief look at spinning sock yarns in *Yarns* (p. 107) completes the picture.

—Elaine Rowley

5

Preface

This is a book about knitting, specifically knitting the socks and stockings of the many and varied ethnic groups that reside in the region stretching from the Balkans east to Afghanistan, from the Arab Nations north to Asiatic Russia. Within this region, there has been much strife, with one group at odds with another. Yet, in their rich tradition of knitting, these same people share much. It is this tradition that I have attempted to record.

I have long been fascinated with folk arts, for within this field the crafts were mastered that provided the means for everyday survival. The finest of these handmade goods were greatly embellished to bring beauty into what seems little more than a life of drudgery when viewed from a modern perspective. This I have found to be especially true of the exquisite socks and stockings of the East — there's nothing mundane and ordinary in the lot.

I must stress that this is a book for knitters. There has been no attempt to put together a definitive ethnographic collection of historical significance. I am neither an ethnographer nor historian and am not qualified to present the material within the context of culture.

This book is about knitting — knitting unique and exotic to the western world in both design and structure. Little has been done to record this material, or to make it available to other knitters. Efforts, to date, have been relative to design with, at best, meager attention paid to the craft itself. What survives has been left to hang by the fragile thread of oral tradition. Surely, much has already been lost. Although I have been able to duplicate the techniques, the methods may not be identical to that of the original knitters, only the results.

Let me also state that I am an armchair traveler: I travel the world vicariously through knitting. All the pieces studied here are from

> **"We must take a fresh look at real folkcraft of the past, for it is there that we may find healthy and genuine beauty expressed… [since] the principles that yield beauty in crafts are unchanging and timeless. We do not admire work for the past but because of its enduring present."**
>
> —*THE UNKNOWN CRAFTSMAN by Soetsu Yanagi, 1972*

collections now in this country. My knowledge of the origins is limited to the information from collectors. Some of this information could be erroneous, not only due to language barriers, but also because there has been much movement of peoples within the region. A sample from one area may have its roots in another area.

By no means do I believe that all the possibilities have been covered. After all, this is the work of many individuals from many ethnic groups. In the socks and stockings I have studied, no two pair are alike — and I am not just referring to appearances. Structurally, each pair studied fits within a general mode, yet none are identical. This is true both throughout the region and within specific groups in a locale. To the casual eye, socks may appear to be the same, but many methods have been used to produce a similar result.

It is my hope that readers will be able to apply this prolific material not only to footwear, but also to their other knitting projects.

My work stresses the craft of knitting, not the art. Before becoming an artisan, one must master the craft. Since knitting's roots do not stretch into the far reaches of antiquity, much of the design of what is knit originates elsewhere. This is true of these socks and stockings. Initially the designs were knitted interpretations of other folk arts that developed earlier, especially weaving. But with the passing of generations, the origins and meanings of the designs have blurred and become more specific to knitting.

In stressing the craft rather than the art, I do not mean to denigrate the art. Rather, I am aware that the art lies elsewhere; it comes from within the artisan. Armed with the techniques and exposed to representative pieces, knitters can create within the tradition rather than follow a specific pattern. My goal is to give knitters this means to stretch themselves to greater creativity.

—Priscilla A. Gibson-Roberts

A unique approach to knitting and knitted footwear developed in the region stretching from the Balkans east to Afghanistan, from the Arab Nations north to Asiatic Russia.

Historical Roots 1

Knitting is a humble craft, easily pursued by people of all walks of life. The necessary tools are negligible: yarn and a set of two or more needles, pointed at one or both ends. The process is simple, consisting of little more than forming interlocking loops from a continuous strand of yarn.

But, for all its simplicity, knitting is not an ancient craft. The oldest known piece of true knitting, a fragment of a sock found in Egypt, dates somewhere between 800-1000 AD. Earlier samples, previously thought to be knitting, are now believed to be a form of knotless netting worked with a single threaded needle using numerous short lengths of yarn.

The resulting fabric appears to be 'cross-stitch' knitting — a similarity that has often confused those studying the origins of knitting. While the 'open' knit stitch is easily recognizable, the 'crossed' knit stitch must be carefully studied before one can ascertain how it was constructed.

Even all knitting is not the same. In the cradle of knitting, early needles had hooked ends. This explains why Eastern knits and purls are formed differently. As is often the case, a combined method has advantages.

Let's begin with the stitches — how they are formed, how they sit on the needle, the stitch structure.

9

Illustrations

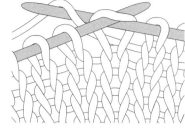

1

Western knit
The yarn is wrapped front to back over right needle tip; the new stitch loop's leading side is on the front of the needle.

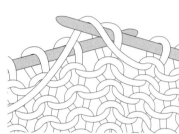

Western purl
The yarn is wrapped front to back over right needle tip; the new stitch loop's leading side is on the front of the needle.

10

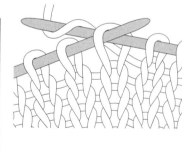

2

Eastern knit
The yarn is wrapped back to front over right needle tip; the new stitch loop's leading side is on the back of the needle.

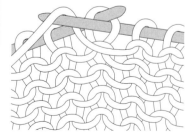

Eastern purl
The yarn is wrapped back to front over right needle tip; the new stitch loop's leading side is on the back of the needle.

Stitch structure

Mary Thomas's Knitting Book defines the various knit structures by the way the stitch sits on the needle (the stitch mount) as Western and Eastern techniques, plus a combined method practiced in much of Eastern Europe where influences overlap. How the yarn is carried in the hand, whether in the right or in the left, is insignificant. The differences result from how the existing stitch is entered with the working needle and the direction the yarn is wrapped around this needle to form the new stitch. And, in each case, the resulting stitch may be *open* or *crossed*. Understanding stitch mount and the choices it provides is vital to mastery of the craft.

As stated, the knit fabric is created of interlocking loops from a continuous strand of yarn. An initial set of loops is cast onto a needle. Thereafter, each new stitch is formed by first entering a loop in the former row, wrapping the yarn on the needle, and drawing a new loop through. Each loop has two sides, a leading side (right arm) and a trailing side (left arm).

How the yarn is wrapped on the needle determines how the new loop (stitch) will be mounted on the needle:

1 If the yarn is wrapped from front to back, the loop's leading side will be on the front of the needle (Western knitting: the standard American method).

2 If wrapped from back to front, the loop's leading side will be on the back of the needle (Eastern knitting).

3 If stockinette stitch is being worked and the yarn is wrapped from front to back for the knit (Western) and from back to front for the purl stitch (Eastern), the leading side of the new loop will be on the front when forming a knit stitch and on the back of the needle when forming a purl stitch (combined knitting).

How a loop is entered when forming a new stitch will determine if that existing stitch will be a standard (open) stitch or a twisted (crossed) stitch.

4 When the position of the leading side of the loop is retained (knit through the front of the loop for Western), a standard (open) stitch results.

5 When the position of the leading/trailing sides of the loop are transposed, a twisted (crossed) stitch results. The twisted stitch will have a left cross in Western knitting; in Eastern knitting, it will have a right cross. Since in combined knitting the existing loops can have the leading side either on the front or the back, it can cross in either direction.

Eastern and Western knitting are mirror image techniques. Combined knitting is seen by some as the best of both worlds — if one has a command of the intricacies of stitch mount. The wrap of both the Western knit stitch and the Eastern purl stitch requires the same length of yarn to form the stitch; the yarn travels in a straight line from the last stitch formed to the wrap of the new stitch. (Conversely, the Eastern knit stitch and Western purl stitch also use the same length of yarn, but in this case, the yarn travels at an angle across the needle from the last stitch formed, thus requiring more yarn to wrap the new stitch.) The significance of the length of yarn required in forming a stitch is apparent when knitting stockinette flat or in knit/purl textured design: combining the Western knit stitch and the Eastern purl stitch can insure that both stitches are worked at the same gauge.

Methods

Familiarity with the tools used also helps in understanding the difference in Eastern and Western methods. Historically in Northern and Western Europe, knitting was worked on sets of straight needles, pointed at both ends, while in the Balkans and the Middle East, the needles were traditionally hooked at one end. A hooked needle made the Eastern purl stitch effortless. In fact, in many locales, color-stranded designs were worked purl side facing with the yarn tensioned around the neck. Since only a flick of the thumb was required to position the yarn for the hook to

carry it through the loop, incredible speeds could be reached with designs in many colors. This method of knitting has all but died out within the region. (Although, interestingly, it is still a common method among the indigenous peoples of much of South America.) Not only did the hooked needle facilitate the knitting, but it also allowed the freedom to move between knitting and a form of crochet within the same project, greatly increasing artistic expression.

The combined method, with or without the hooked needle, is still practiced today; the Eastern method is seldom seen. In this country, the Western technique is the standard method, and other methods are relegated to obscurity. This is a loss, for all techniques offer options and are ethnically significant.

Not only do differences exist between Eastern and Western knitting techniques, but the approach to the construction of socks and stockings differs dramatically. It begins with the number of needles used. In Great Britain and North America, the usual method requires the use of three needles to hold the stitches with a fourth working needle. Knitters in Northern and Eastern Europe and the Middle East have traditionally divided the stitches on four needles with a fifth working needle. Since half the stitches are for the back of the leg/heel/sole with the other half for the front of the leg/instep, the latter method is

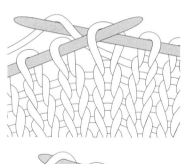

3

Combined knit
The yarn is wrapped front to back over needle tip. Note that leading side of loop is on back of left needle, and leading side of loop is on front of right needle.

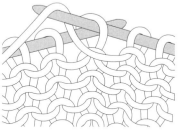

Combined purl
The yarn is wrapped back to front. Note that leading side of loop is on front of left needle and leading side of loop is on back of right needle.

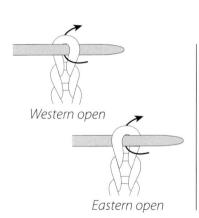

Western open

Eastern open

4

For a standard (open, untwisted) stitch, work into the leading side of the loop.

11

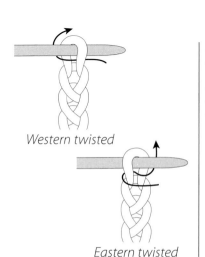

Western twisted

Eastern twisted

5

For a twisted (crossed) stitch, work into the trailing side of the loop. In Western knitting, the stitch will cross to the left; in Eastern knitting, to the right.

6

Which is the sock? All, of course. A Western sock folds along the center back 'seam,' revealing the familiar profile, RIGHT— an Eastern sock masquerading as a Western one.

Eastern socks fold along the sides, emphasizing the front, LEFT, and back, RIGHT. This is how you will see these socks charted and photographed. But thanks to the elasticity of knitting, the differences fade when the socks are worn.

more practical. Working with sets of five needles is gaining widespread acceptance in the United States as knitters have become aware that dividing the stitches on four needles eliminates the need to rearrange the needles when turning the heel.

But the difference in construction is much more dramatic. In fact, the approach is exactly opposite. The Western sock is cast on at the top (cuff) and worked down the leg to the heel. No shaping is required for socks, but when of stocking length, the leg is shaped to the contour of the calf with decreases at each side of the center back. This 'seam' is a dominant feature of the stockings. Turning the heel is typically a three-step process beginning with (1) a heel flap worked over the back half of the stitches, (2) a heel base which, by one means or another, joins the sides of the heel flap and (3) side gussets which return the work into a circle for the foot. The foot is knit to the desired length and decreased by some means for the toe.

The Eastern sock begins at the toe and is increased for the foot. In most cases, on reaching the ankle, heel stitches are set aside and the knitting continues up the leg to the bind-off at the top. Socks require no leg shaping, while stockings are discreetly increased within the pattern of the calf portion, invisible to the eye. After the completion of the foot and leg, the heel is inserted into stitches from the sole and leg back. The heel is

worked circularly out from the sock, decreasing to provide the proper shape.

6 Socks made by these two methods look very different. The Western way, with its center back 'seam,' has two sides, a feature often emphasized in historical pieces with a 'clock' (a design essentially outlining the gusset) at the ankle. The Western sock or stocking lies flat sideways, its outline matching the contours of the leg and foot. The Eastern sock, with no center back seam, has a front and back, a feature often emphasized by motif placement or vertical side borders. It lies flat front to back, becoming a tube with a pointed toe (heel extension on backside).

The craft

The earliest known knitting was a sock knitted in the Eastern way. Thus, the region is recognized as the cradle of knitting. Although believed to portray an early period in the craft, these socks suggest a fairly mature craft. The color-stranded patterns are as desirable today as they were nearly a thousand years ago.

With the importance of Eastern socks and stockings to the craft, why do we in the West know so little about them? For the average knitter, access is limited to three works published in English: Kenan Ozbel's *Knitted Stockings from Turkish Villages* (out of print), Betsy Harrell's *Anatolian Knitting Designs*, and Anna

Zilboorg's *Fancy Feet* — none of which detail the craft. Furthermore, little has been done within the region to preserve the craft. Some information has been recorded in the Balkans (none translated into English), but again, all emphasis has been on the art, not the craft. The craft has been abandoned to the whims of oral tradition, not dependable when the need for the craft is no longer viable. Luckily, there are collections, both here and abroad. Much can be resurrected from these socks and stockings, but more is on the verge of extinction if not already gone.

The socks and stockings were very important in the peasant culture of this region, just as mittens were to the peasants of Northern Europe, from the Baltic States throughout Scandinavia. When looking at the work of this vast region spanning a range of cultures and many ethnic groups, we see tremendous diversity. Generalizations are difficult to make, but the importance of the socks and stockings is universal. They played a particularly significant role in the marriage ceremonies of the various cultures whether in Bulgaria, Turkey, or Georgia. The creation of the socks and stockings, their display, and exchange were a central part of these celebrations.

Without the dazzling designs, whether geometric, stylized, or representational, the craft would not have reached a high level of significance; the art and craft are intrinsically united.

That many of the designs were symbolic at some point is of little doubt. They were the creations of an illiterate people who used symbols to convey information. In the 20th century, this has changed dramatically. Only in rural areas is the craft diligently pursued — and even there, it is threatened as the modern world encroaches upon the agrarian world. The stockings and their designs no longer mean what they meant to former generations. Regardless, even today the stockings are more than just a folk art to be collected; they are a part of the heritage. Betsy Harrell states it best in *Anatolian Knitting Designs*: "The stockings are needed to keep the feet warm, but the motifs the knitter decorates them with are another matter. The patterns are products of both her inventive imagination and her heritage. They provide an outlet for the artistic creativity she is capable of, and they keep her traditions in her heart and her village."

For knitters dedicated to their craft, all knitting, regardless of its national and/or ethnic origins, is part of our common heritage. The distinctive techniques and sumptuous design development of this region offers much to the Western sock knitter. But they can be used for much more than the reproduction of socks and stockings. Specifically, the invisible *two-needle cast on* can be used in making pouches, mittens, and gloves. Gloves in both Turkey and Afghanistan are worked in this manner, a new cast on for each digit, united for the hand. In Iran, caps often have a little topknot begun in this manner. The *circular cast on* for the *tufted toe* could make a special beginning for a child's cap. The *two-needle cast on* offers potential for lace knitters who are interested in circular pieces. The ability to incorporate intarsia-type motifs, often believed possible only in flat knitting, into a circular structure has countless applications: mittens, caps, even sweaters — but especially Christmas stockings. Possibilities abound, limited only by one's imagination.

13

Visual excitement reflects knitting excitement. Here the variously-patterned
sole, instep, heel, and ankle meet. A glance at the facing page puts
the intersecting patterns of these Macedonian socks in context.

Socks and Stockings 2

With an understanding of the background of the craft, the next step is developing an appreciation of the art. Socks and stockings are the canvases on which hand-crafters of this region made their artistic expressions.

The region is vast, the art is highly varied, but some generalizations can be drawn regarding the sizes and shapes of these canvases as well as the principal ways the designs are developed.

After a brief overview, it's on to the real socks and stockings — twenty six pair that make up our knitter's collection. We will show the stockings from several angles, turn them over, even show some from the side as we would a Western sock. They were made to be worn, and many do show signs of wear. But mostly they show a varied style of knitting, rich in both design and technique.

Patterns and charts

Basic lengths

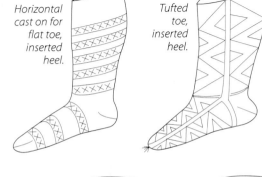

Anklet

Sock

Stocking

Basic shapes

Horizontal cast on for flat toe, inserted heel.

Tufted toe, inserted heel.

Vertical cast on with toe depth, side and seam stitches, inserted heel.

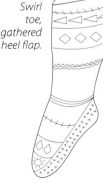

Swirl toe, gathered heel flap.

Basic lengths and shapes

1 Length of leg differentiates the three styles: the anklet, a short sock extending just above the ankle; the sock, a longer one extending only to the base of the calf, thus requiring no shaping; and the stocking, a much greater length that requires increasing to accommodate the contours of the leg. Stockings can extend up to the knee or beyond.

2 The shape of the sock depends on the construction elements selected. There are many toe and heel combinations, all affecting the ultimate appearance of the sock. The accompanying illustrations show basic shapes that can be expected from some of the combinations possible.

Design development

As with length and shape, certain generalizations can be made about design development. Some designs might crop up anywhere within the region, but certain styles are associated with specific regions and/or ethnic groups.

Attention to detail by Eastern knitters differs from that of Western knitters. In the Middle East, truncating a vertical pattern when the desired length is reached is common; many Western knitters would spend hours planning the placement of pattern to end at a specific position. Little concern for incomplete repeats at the end of horizontal bands is also quite common in Eastern knitting. Culture differs considerably from East to West, and art is an expression of culture. To the Eastern eye, severing a pattern, vertically or horizontally, does nothing to diminish the beauty of the object. Furthermore, many of the knitters were illiterate, working the patterns from some inner vision rather than by carefully calculating and charting to make everything fit. Moving westward to a more literate population, one finds more attention paid to the little details: complete repeats, positioning the join of the round at the inside of the leg thus necessitating a right and left sock, working in all ends on the inside, etc.

3 Horizontal bands of patterning encircling the foot and leg are typical of much of the Balkans. The bands are both geometric and representational types of designs. Many of the socks of this region are of cotton yarns as well as the more typical wool yarns. Farther north and east in Georgia, horizontal bands depict highly stylized flora and fauna in combination with geometric designs. Often these socks are created with very fine yarns in silk as well as wool.

4 In much of the Middle East, the patterning is limited to geometric or highly abstract forms since the dominant religious beliefs ban the depiction of living forms. Here we see a lot of vertical development of pattern, often in mirror image from side to side. This patterning may be developed on a solid ground in a single contrast color or the design may be the solid color with the ground in bands of several contrasting colors. In some cases, particularly among some of the older pieces, the designs are a multi-colored development with no specific ground color. Many of the older pieces are worked in a very hairy, scratchy wool yarn.

5 Some of the nomadic people of the Middle East, including the Kurds, Bakhtiari, and Lur, use natural white and other natural colors for textured patterning. Some patterning closely resembles the simple knit-purl designs of early British fisherman sweaters; others use two-end knitting techniques and traveling stitches reminiscent of the work of Scandinavia and Bavaria. It is interesting to note that many of these peoples make their socks of a wonderfully soft, lustrous, long-staple wool that would be a delight to wear.

Although not common, simple lace patterns in vertical columns in natural white yarns are seen in parts of the Middle East. With the looser fit of the socks, lace patterns often do not realize their full potential as a design element.

6 Framed abstract designs are favored in much of Iran, especially to the north and along the Caspian Sea. This region favors a looser gauge in the knitting than most others within the area. The wool is fairly coarse, yet one with a good hand and nice luster. The colors are brilliant: intense purple with natural beige and gray or hot pink with cranberry red being highly favored. Both combinations have bright accents of red, teal, yellow, and green.

Throughout the area one sees an occasional footed pattern: geometric patterning intensely developed on the foot up to the ankle with a plain natural white leg. In some cases, the leg portion might have simple cabling or vertical lace patterning.

3

LEFT Horizontal bands in geometric patterns. *RIGHT* Horizontal bands with stylized flowers and birds.

4

LEFT Vertical columns in mirror image in contrast color on solid ground. *RIGHT* Vertical pattern on changing ground color.

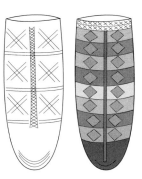

5

LEFT Simple textured patterning. *RIGHT* Vertical multi-colored patterning.

17

6

LEFT Framed pattern of abstract designs. *RIGHT* Footed pattern with plain leg.

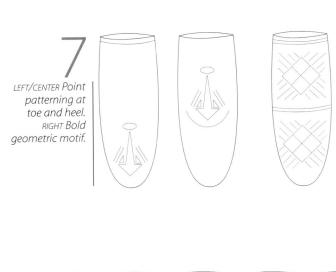

7 LEFT/CENTER *Point patterning at toe and heel.* RIGHT *Bold geometric motif.*

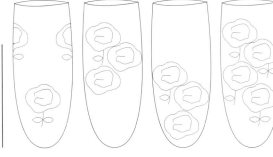

8 *Floral patterns on — LEFT to RIGHT: instep and sides of leg; leg front; instep; entire front.*

9 *Inserted heel patterns*

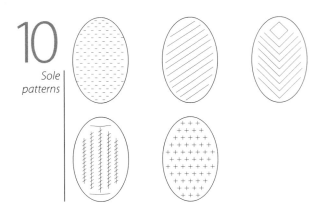

10 *Sole patterns*

7 Point patterning can be found as far west as the Balkans but is also typical of Turkey. In this case, the main pattern is developed on the top of the toe, extending up toward the instep. This pattern, or a similar complementary one, is also positioned on the back of the inserted heel or above the gathered heel flap. It is usually in bright colors against a ground of white for women and, in some cases, black for men.

Geometric motifs in brilliant colors, often located prominently on the instep and leg, are favored by some in Bosnia. Much of the patterning is worked in *Bosnian crochet,* often in combination with a knitted sole. These socks are quite boot-like in appearance.

8 In Bulgaria and along the Dalmatian Coast there is a special type of motif knitting. The motifs are most often beautifully depicted floral patterns. This patterning is usually associated with flat knitting, yet here it is executed circularly in socks and stockings. These are very elegant stockings. The Western knitter might wonder that much of the motif is hidden under the shoe; but these glorious socks were often worn with slipper-type shoes when outdoors, without shoes when indoors.

9 On any of the aforementioned, inserted heel patterns can play a major role in design. The bottom of the heel is often a continuation of the sole pattern with a contrasting design on the heel back. In other cases, the heel back is an extension of the back leg pattern. Or, the heel may be a complementary design to the other patterns. And occasionally, the heel is a gaudy contrast to the rest of the sock. The importance of heel patterning should not be underestimated, especially in a region where clogs and sandals are traditional footwear.

10 For some in this area, the sole pattern is also important. Where horizontal bands or overall patterning is used, the sole usually maintains the same pattern as the instep. But in many of the other styles, the sole is worked in a small, simple geometric pattern. Again, since many of the socks and stockings were worn indoors without shoes, the importance of the patterning on the sole becomes clear: when the wearer is seated, the soles are often exposed to the view of others.

Chapter 2

Selected samples and charts

This is not an ethnographic collection organized by ethnic group or region. It is a knitter's collection. Samples were selected on the basis of knitting technique; some techniques relate to the construction of a sock, others to the design. In the final analysis, the process was arbitrary and highly personal.

Every attempt was made to identify the samples by ethnic group and/or country of origin. This information is as correct as the memory of the collector or the accession cards and/or cataloging of museum collections. Considerable overlap exists, with the same sock or stockings found in widely dispersed areas within this vast region. After all, emigration of individuals and groups has been significant throughout the area. Furthermore, the homelands of the various ethnic groups were seldom considered when national boundaries were established.

When using the charts for the various pieces, do not disregard the old ethnic concept of fit. Taken as a group, these socks and stockings are most suited to a looser fit. Traditionally they are not designed to follow precisely the contours of the leg and foot. They should be knitted with considerable ease incorporated. The amount of ease is directly related to firmness of gauge and length of stranding yarns: the tighter the knitting and the longer the stranding, the greater the required ease. They might require from 15% to as much as 25% ease for the elaborately color-stranded patterns, while the textured and motif patterns might need 10% or less ease for a traditional fit.

When compared to modern, Western knitting, the row and stitch gauge are unusual. In many cases, there is not much difference between the width of the stitch and the depth of the row. This is, in part, due to the common practice of knitting with the dense, worsted-type handspun yarns and firm gauge. In addition, many of the color-stranded patterns contain strong diagonal design elements. As a result, the knit stitch becomes more square than might be anticipated. Therefore, many of the charts are shown accurately on a square grid. Others are presented best on a typical knitter's grid.

Although every attempt has been made to retain the integrity of the original, the charts are designed for use. More often than not, the charts are a composite of the pair since seldom are the two socks identical. Also, when obvious errors have occurred in the original, they have been corrected on the charts. If the crafting has been somewhat haphazard, it too has been refined within the bounds of the accepted techniques of the region. Socks and stockings can thus be reproduced from the written information and charts, the only necessary adaptation being that of size.

In the sock descriptions, the italics denote techniques fully detailed in subsequent chapters. They are listed in the index for easy reference.

Using the charts

Charts are worked in stockinette stitch unless otherwise indicated. For assistance in reading charted stitch patterns, turn to page 116. The few standard knitting abbreviations used are listed there. We have described ribbing patterns as 2/2, 1/2, etc. Generally the first number applies to the knit stitches, the second to the purls.

19

1

Mamluk socks of Egypt

Descendants of the Mongols, the Mamluks, knit these socks sometime in the 11th-14th centuries. Knitting was no longer in its infancy as proved by the skills necessary to both shape and embellish with multi-colored designs. Both socks are knit of handspun, 2-ply cotton in natural white and shades of indigo blue. One is worked to a gauge of 12 stitches and 14 rows to the inch, and its patterned bands are an Arabic inscription repeating the word 'Allah.' The other sock is knit at 10 stitches and 13 rows to the inch, and its bands simulate an Arabic inscription. Knit in the classic Eastern structure, they begin at the toe with a fairly wide section (*vertical cast on*) that has the tail looped around to draw in the excess fullness. The toe is increased randomly to the full width of the foot, the knitting continues to the heel where stitches are placed on hold while the knitting continues up the leg. The heel is a shallow *inserted heel*, shaped with decreases.

20

☐ *Natural*
☐ *Indigo blue*

Foot

└─ *8 st rep* ─┘

└─ *13st rep* ─┘

Leg

└─ *13st rep* ─┘

This early 20th century pair of striped Bulgarian socks proves that wonderful does not necessarily equate with difficult, for this pair is simplicity itself. They are worked at a gauge of 7 stitches and 9 rows to the inch in alternate stripes of plied cotton yarns (black, white, and gold) and plied wool yarns (red and green). The gold and white stripes are both three rounds deep while the others are four rounds deep.

The sock begins at the toe with a *horizontal cast on* of eight stitches over two needles. The toe is increased on every other round to the desired size and knit to the heel. Here, a *waste yarn technique* is appropriate, positioned in the middle of a 4-round stripe. The leg is continued to the desired length, culminating with a purl round, a round of eyelets, and the bound off edge.

A twisted cord is made of the tail yarn with a second color, knotted at the end with an overhand knot. This is laced through the eyelets as a tie.

The heel is inserted after the removal of the waste yarn. The final two rounds of the 4-round stripe and another 4 rounds are worked before decreases begin on every round. Notice that the color sequence is continued in reverse order on the heel. The final few heel stitches are laced and drawn together. Simple, yet charming.

2
Striped
Bulgarian
socks

21

3
Bakhtiari stockings

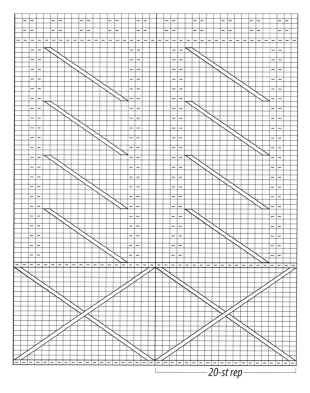

20-st rep

☐ Knit ▨ 1/1 RC
⊟ Purl ◩ 1/1 LC

These stockings, circa 1970, are from the Bakhtiari, a nomadic group in Iran. The stockings are knit of a hand-spun 2-ply wool, worked to a gauge of 10 stitches and 10 rows to the inch. The yarn is handspun of a silky, lustrous wool in natural white. The entire foot, up to the pattern bands above the ankle, is worked in *two-end knitting*.

The stockings are begun with a *vertical cast on* of ten stitches. These initial stitches wrap around the toes as the girth is increased on each side on every round. Four rounds after increasing has begun, a decorative 4-stitch ridge is created on the top of the instep. To create this ridge, four stitches (two at the end of the right needle, two at the beginning of the left needle)

22

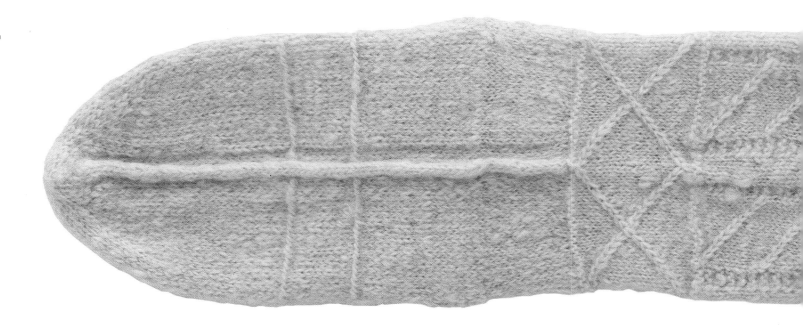

are worked from one ball, the yarn drawn tightly across the back from the other ball, and the two-end knitting resuming thereafter. Two *twined knit* stitch rows are positioned one inch apart on the instep only.

Upon reaching the heel position, the sole stitches are placed on hold and the back leg stitches are cast on with a *backward loop cast on* using both yarns alternately. A 4-stitch ridge is also positioned at the center back. One and a half inches above the opening for the heel, knitting continues with one yarn only. Two bands of *traveling stitch* patterns are followed by a 2/2 rib (two knit stitches and two garter stitches in place of the typical purl stitches). The top is bound off, and the yarn broken off and allowed to hang free.

The heel stitches are picked up and worked, maintaining the center back ridge down to the point of the heel. Decreasing begins immediately after the pickup of stitches. The decreases occur within 10-stitch side panels to match the toe. When all but the panel stitches have been decreased, the remaining stitches are grafted.

4
Lur
Socks

Side panel

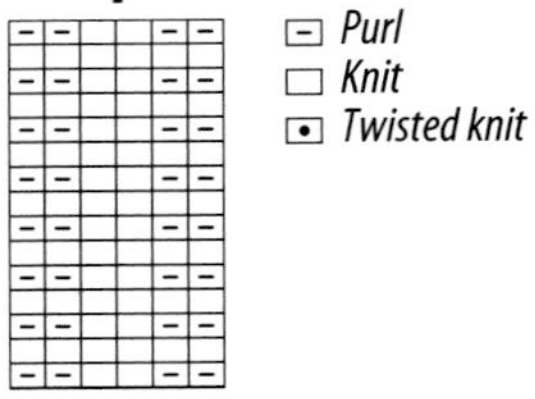

- ⊟ Purl
- ☐ Knit
- ⊡ Twisted knit

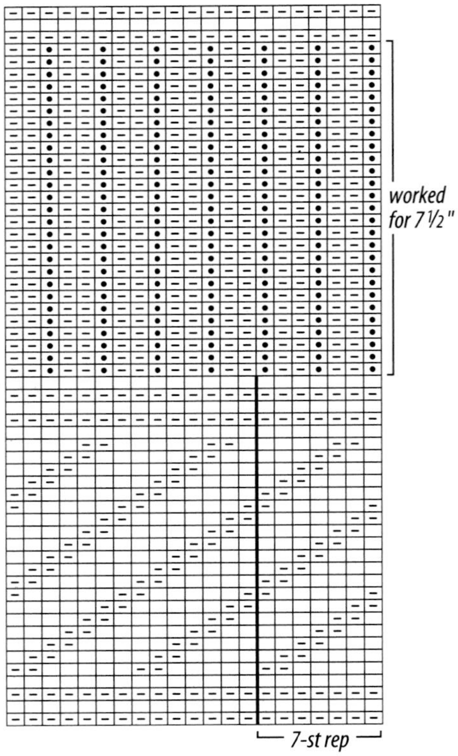

worked
for 7½"

⌊— 7-st rep —⌋

The Lur, a nomadic group in Iran, are highly skilled spinners and knitters, as shown by these socks. The yarn is a 2-ply handspun of natural white medium wool. These socks are quite simple, but very elegant. Begun at the toe, the side panel is worked in a simple textured pattern of garter stitch on each side of two central stockinette stitches. This pattern outlines the stockinette foot, divides to continue both up the leg and down the *inserted heel*. Just above the ankle, simple knit-purl diagonals form a horizontal band topped by 7½ inches of a 1/2 rib, worked with the knit stitches *twisted*. The heel is inserted and decreased on every round until all the stockinette stitches have been decreased. The final six side panel stitches are grafted.

A combination of commercial yarns (acrylic and cotton) and handspun, hand-dyed wool is used in these northeast Iranian/Afghani socks, circa 1970. They are gauged at 5.5 stitches and 7 rows to the inch. The *two-color vertical cast on* is maintained as a side panel through the heel but not up the leg. The sock is worked to the heel and divided. Since there are no vertical patterns to maintain, the *waste yarn technique* is suitable for this heel. The leg is increased in pattern, ending with a purl round and bind off. The waste yarn is removed and the heel inserted.

Heel

5

Northeast Iranian/ Afghani socks

- ■ Charcoal
- □ Light orange
- ■ Dark orange
- ■ Purple
- □ Green
- ■ Dark green
- ■ Wine red
- ■ Light blue
- ■ Dark Navy
- ▬ Purl
- ● Heel

7

Iranian shepherd socks

Embroidery: **A.** *4 rows charcoal with outline stitch in teal, pink, red/white, and green.* **B.** *4 rows charcoal with outline stitch in green, red/white, pink, and teal.* **C.** *With red and pink held together, purl last round .*

28

In an area known for its hot pink/cranberry red socks, this particular pair of Iranian shepherd socks, circa 1970, is unique in its clever use of the materials at hand. On the upper portion of the leg, where several bands of *Bosnian crochet* are worked, the white accent is not a true yarn. It is a strip of white nylon tricot fabric! With this one notable exception, these socks are knitted of handspun 2-ply yarn at a gauge of 6 stitches and 7 rows to the inch.

Everything else is traditional, beginning with the *two-color cast on* at the toe. The increases at the toe are contained within the side panels. At the heel, the sole stitches were put on hold while back leg stitches were cast on with a *backward loop cast on*. This allows patterns to match when worked in the reverse direction for the *inserted heel*. Small sections of color are worked in *zigzag intarsia*. The top of the sock is bound off in a double strand of yarn, working with both the hot pink and cranberry red at the same time. Colored tails from the band below, including the nylon tricot, are drawn through the final stitch to form a pseudo tassel.

The heel is picked up and worked down, altering the pattern to fit within the frame of the side panels. The side panel stitches are also decreased several times, ending with the final few stitches drawn together into a point.

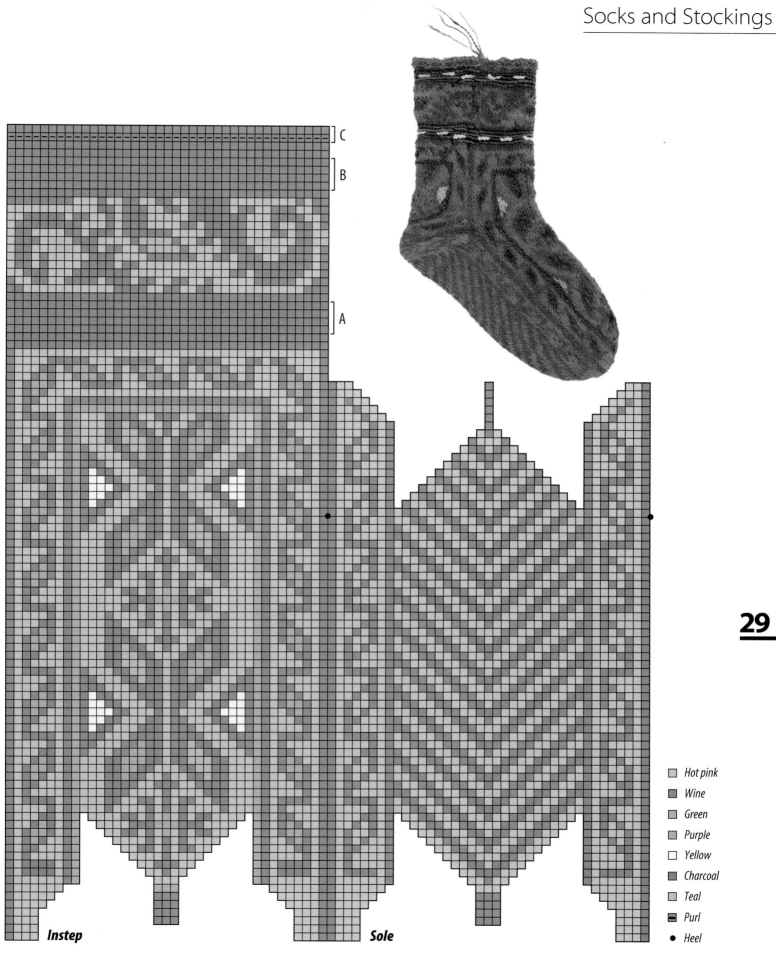

] C

] B

] A

29

Instep

Sole

☐ Hot pink
▨ Wine
▨ Green
▨ Purple
☐ Yellow
▨ Charcoal
▨ Teal
▰ Purl
• Heel

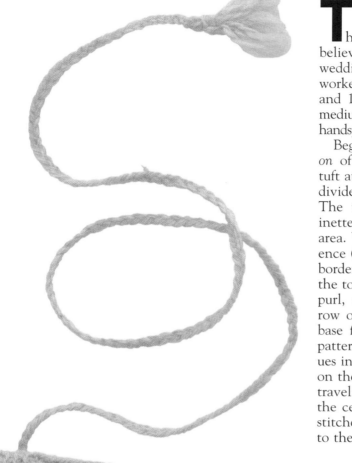

This wonderful old pair is believed to be a Turkish man's wedding stockings. They are worked at a gauge of 10 stitches and 12 rows to the inch in a medium weight 2-ply yarn, handspun from a long, luster wool.

Beginning with a *circular cast on* of eight stitches around a tuft at the toe, the stitches are divided into a *four-unit swirl*. The toe is worked in stockinette throughout the increase area. When the full circumference (96 stitches) is reached, a border pattern is worked across the top of the foot (one row of purl, one row of eyelets, one row of purl). This serves as a base for a traveling stitch rib pattern. While the sole continues in stockinette, the pattern on the instep is a 6/1 rib, with traveling stitches worked over the center four of the six knit stitches. The foot is continued to the desired length. The sole stitches are worked in *waste yarn* for the *inserted heel*, then the border pattern is repeated, this time on all the stitches.

The leg is increased by 2 stitches and the rib pattern is resumed; 14 repeats encircle the leg. The leg ends with a 3-row border of *Bosnian single crochet*, a fourth round worked as 3 slip stitches, chain-3 picot loop, ending in a long 3-strand braid and tassel for a tie.

After removal of the waste yarn, the heel is worked below the eyelet band. The heel back is worked in traveling stitch rib, the sole in stockinette stitch. The decreases are offset from the edge by two stitches, thus creating a side panel of stitches. Decreases begin immediately and are worked on every round. When only the side panel stitches remain, they are bound off together.

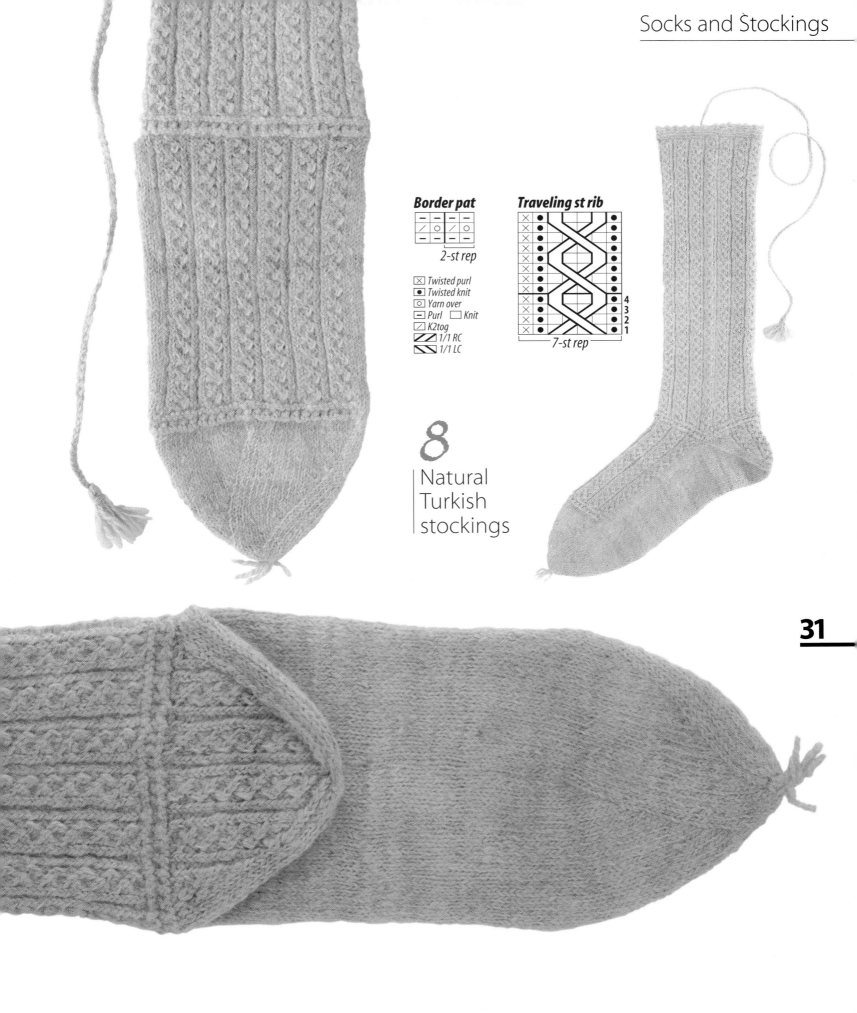

Border pat

2-st rep

⊠ Twisted purl
• Twisted knit
○ Yarn over
− Purl ☐ Knit
⧄ K2tog
▧ 1/1 RC
▨ 1/1 LC

Traveling st rib

7-st rep

8

Natural
Turkish
stockings

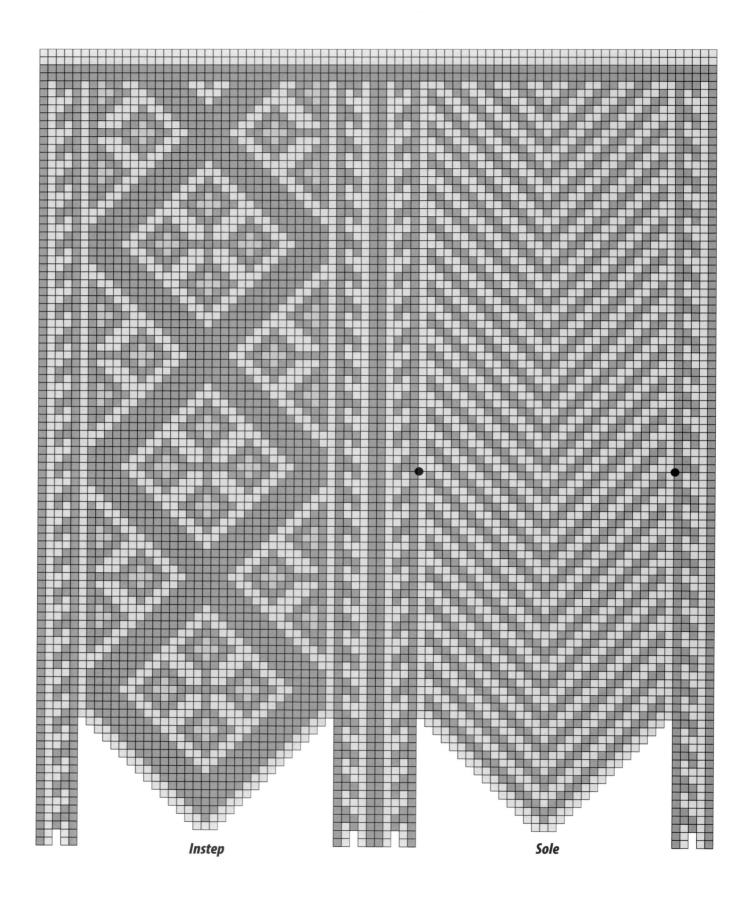

Instep

Sole

Chapter 2

These socks were purchased in Isfahan, Iran, in 1976. They are knit of handspun, 2-ply yarn from a *dual-coated sheep*. The yarn is somewhat hairy, but not unpleasant to the hand.

The socks begin with a vertical *two-color cast on*. (An interesting feature is the wrapping of the tail yarn around the cast on.) The foot is worked to the heel where the sole stitches are put on hold and the back leg *cast on with backward loops* to allow the vertical matching of color. The leg ends with a knit round followed by two rounds of *Bosnian slip stitch crochet*. The design portions in contrast colors are worked in *zigzag intarsia*.

The heel is most interesting since it does not match the rest of the sock even in stitch count: the extra stitches picked up to close the heel gap are not immediately decreased. The yarns used for the heel are more crudely spun, the knitting more crudely executed. Even the colors are not a match. Possibly the heel, being a small section easily replaced, was turned over to a child for completion? This approach was not uncommon as a means to give a child experience without the sometimes overwhelming challenge of knitting an entire sock.

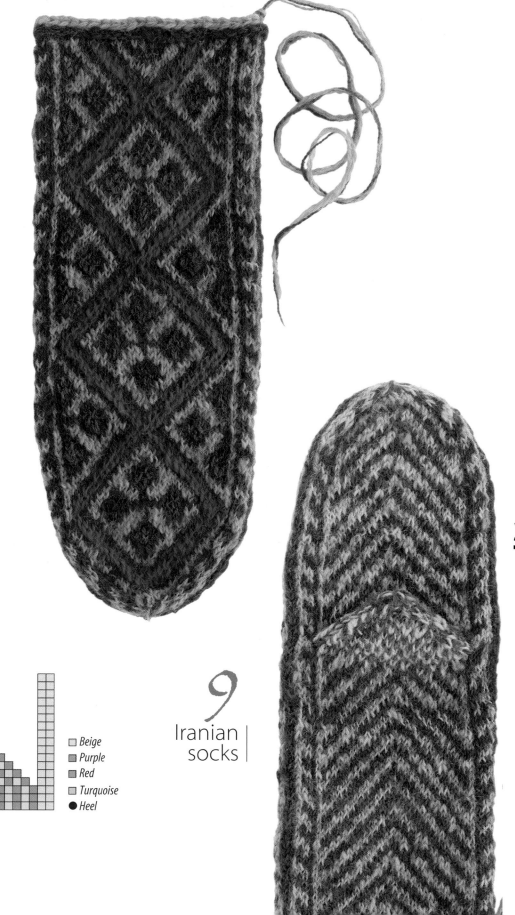

Heel

☐ Beige
▨ Purple
▨ Red
▨ Turquoise
● Heel

9
Iranian socks

33

10 | Ukrainian socks

Not quite Eastern, not quite Western, these socks are the product of overlapping influences in the Carpathian Mountains. They are the festive socks of the Hutzel women.

In Western fashion, they begin at the top and are worked down through the heel to the toe. But the round begins at the side, not the back leg, thus the jog of color-stranding is in a less visible position between the legs.

A short heel flap is worked back and forth across half the leg stitches. Stitches are picked up along its sides to return to the round, but there are no gussets. In typical Western heels, the heel flap would be longer, thus extra stitches would be picked up along the edges. These stitches must then be removed, creating the gusset. Without the gusset, the Hutzel socks fold forward, not sideways, and fit like Eastern socks.

Each locale has its preferred patterns and colors; the pattern of the color-stranded band at the top of the socks matches the cross-stitch embroidery patterns of the area's blouse. The band is worked in the same fine, plied yarns as the cross-stitch (with the yarns doubled or tripled) at a finer gauge than the sock. In this particular pair, the band is worked at 14 stitches and 14 rows to the inch. The main body of the stockings is knit of two strands of handspun singles at 8 stitches and 10 rows to the inch. The fine wool is used for the patterned band; a silky, luster wool of great durability is used for the main body of the sock. When the patterned band is completed, a round of decreasing is worked to adjust to the larger gauge. This not only insures fit in the sock, but also sets the band off, making it appear folded onto the sock itself.

When the plain portion of the sock is worn out, it can be replaced. Each 'retread' allows further use of the elaborately patterned band and justifies the dedication of time and energy required in its creation. For a closer look at the band, see page 4.

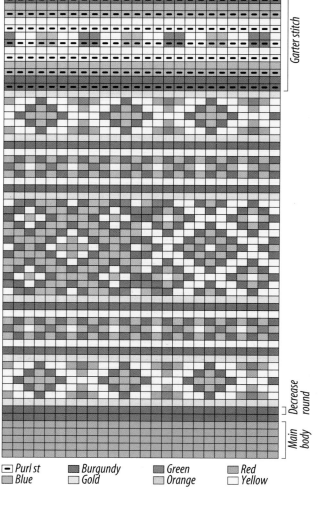

CO

Garter stitch

Decrease round

Main body

| ⊟ Purl st | Burgundy | Green | Red |
| Blue | Gold | Orange | Yellow |

Wool from a *dual-coated sheep* was spun into 2-ply yarn and knit at a gauge of 8 stitches to the inch. A *two-color cast on* of 14 stitches begins the toe. The toe is increased on every round. Worked in a color-stranded pattern, the patterning carries around to the sole and back leg in a mirror image of the instep and front leg. The heel opening is provided with *waste yarn* in a solid color band. The top of the sock ends in a striped 2/2 rib topped with crochet loops. The heel is patterned on back and bottom. Since the heel pattern requires an even number, one additional stitch is added top and bottom.

Heel

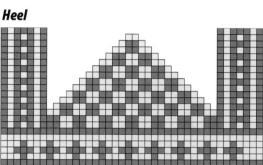

11 | Socks of Iraq

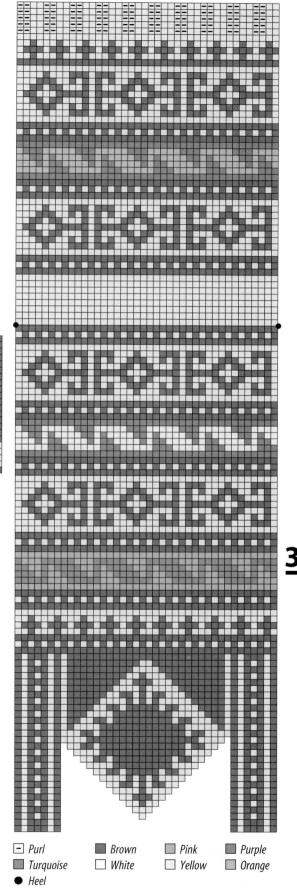

35

- ⊟ Purl
- ▨ Turquoise
- ● Heel
- ▨ Brown
- ☐ White
- ▨ Pink
- ☐ Yellow
- ▨ Purple
- ▨ Orange

36

These Albanian socks are probably a man's wedding socks. The colored handspun singles yarns are of a medium weight, spun from a medium wool. The white yarn is 2-ply cotton. The twist is fairly high on the singles, and 'furrows' appear in the knit structure. Since the twist is properly set, no bias slant is evident. The gauge varies from 7 to 9 stitches and 9 rows to the inch.

To begin, fifteen stitches are cast on over two needles at the toe with a *figure-8 wrap*. This type of sock is somewhat bootlike in appearance so the instep is increased more often than the sole, as in this example. The horizontal patterned band at the point of the toe is not centered, often a result of work done without benefit of a chart. The sole patterning changes when this horizontal band is begun. An instep motif is worked in *zigzag intarsia* because its colors do not carry onto the sole.

The *heel flap* is worked and the cupping of the flap created with *short rows* when the foot is of sufficient length. The initial section of leg above the heel flap is in *Bosnian crochet*, thus stabilizing the shape of the heel. The remainder of that round of the leg is knitted. After 8 rounds, a complementary motif is positioned on the back leg. The remainder of the leg is worked in stockinette stitch and ends with a band of *Bosnian crochet*.

Back Leg

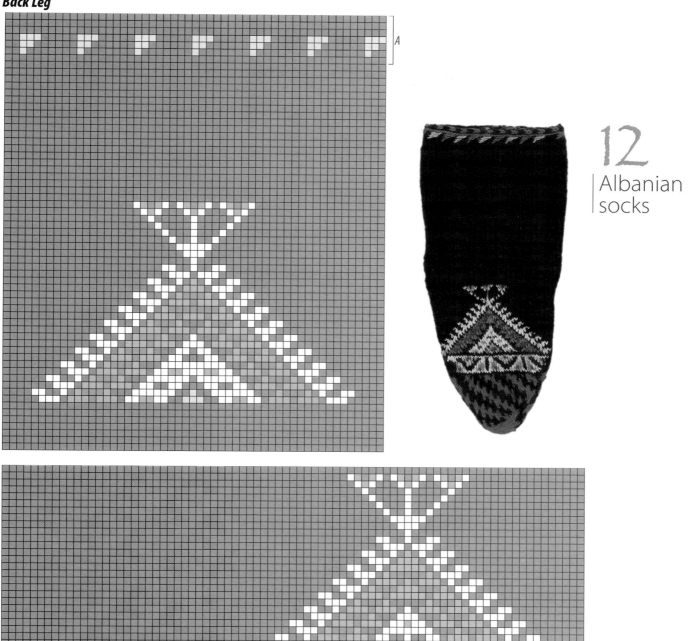

A

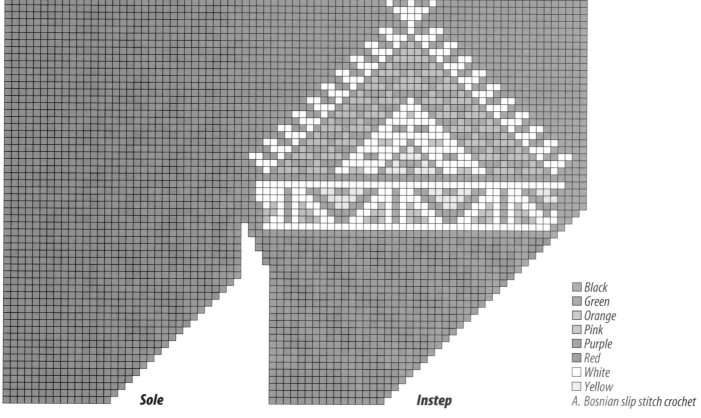

Sole

Instep

12
Albanian
socks

- ☐ Black
- ☐ Green
- ☐ Orange
- ☐ Pink
- ☐ Purple
- ☐ Red
- ☐ White
- ☐ Yellow

A. Bosnian slip stitch crochet

Traditional attire was still a common sight in the Black Sea area when these stockings were purchased around 1960. These stockings are more common in the western reaches of the region and are referred to as Bosnian stockings. The colored yarns are handspun wool singles from a long, luster wool. The white is a 2-ply handspun cotton yarn. Firmly knitted, the gauge varies from 9 to 11 stitches to the inch.

The knit structure was worked in the *Eastern crossed stitch* with bands of *Bosnian crochet* incorporated at intervals. The *two-unit swirl toe* begins with a *backward loop cast on*, worked simultaneously over two needles. A *gathered flap* is worked for the heel. Although beautiful to the eye, the actual construction is somewhat haphazard, with increases occurring irregularly, almost as an afterthought. Shaping varies considerably from one to the other — yet, when on the feet, they appear identical!

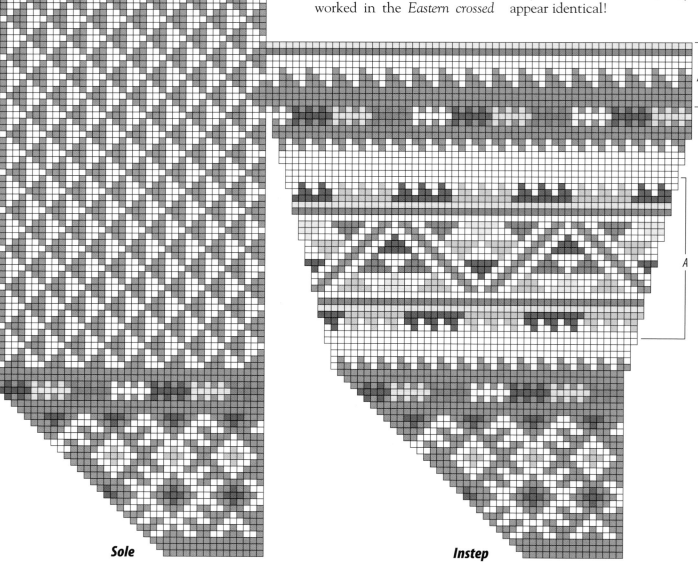

Sole

Instep

Chapter 2

13
Black Sea stockings

■ Green ■ Red ■ Purple
■ Pink □ White □ Yellow
A. Bosnian slip stitch crochet
B. Alternate 1 rnd Bosnian single crochet
and 1 rnd regular slip stitch crochet

Leg

A
A
A
B
A

14

Hennaed stockings of Turkey

Hennaed refers to the use of red in the patterning of these early 20th century stockings, typical of a style worn by both women and girls. This pair is knit of 2-ply handspun wool at a gauge of 7.5 stitches to the inch.

The toe begins with a *striped tubular cast on* in two colors. The *square toe* is used in combination with a tapered foot. Increases are positioned just to the inside of the vertical border pattern. This pattern is a 2/2 cable on a 3-row repeat worked in three colors, white on one side with red and green alternating on the other. The contrast colors are worked in *zigzag intarsia*. At the sides, the vertical stripes are carefully carried up as the work progresses, not chained up as embroidery (although chaining would not be atypical). The sole is plain stockinette.

Upon reaching heel position, the sole stitches were placed on hold and new back leg stitches cast on with a *backward loop*. The leg is continued upward to the horizontal band at the top. This is outlined in black with an embroidered *outline stitch*. The cuff is a 1/1 twisted rib ending in a picot edging: chain-4 picots were worked between each group of 12 stitches bound off; the final section has fewer than 12 stitches. On the next round, the 12-stitch section is chained across, joining at the end into the chain loop of the previous round with a slip stitch. Three chain-4 'petals' are worked into the chain loop.

An *inserted heel* is then worked into the opening. Decreases are worked on every round, positioned on the inside edge of the vertical pattern. The heel has a blunt end worked in red to match the square toe.

Heel

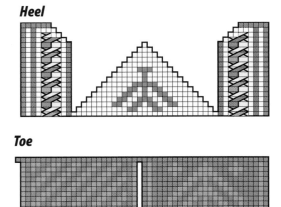

Tubular CO

Toe

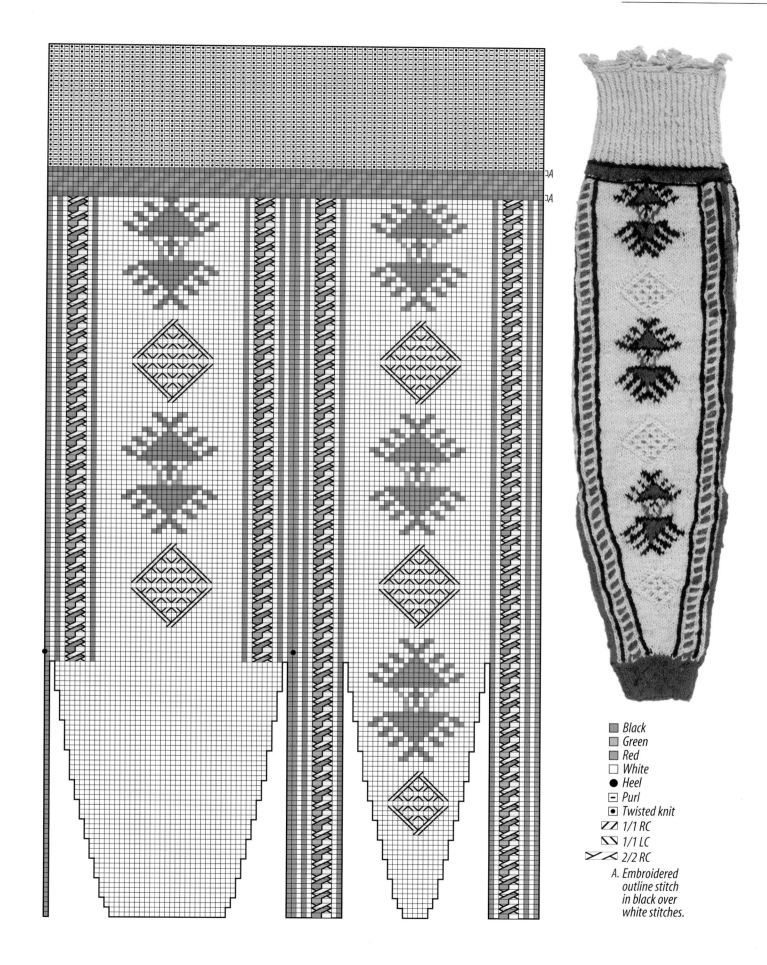

41

- ◼ *Black*
- ◼ *Green*
- ◼ *Red*
- ☐ *White*
- ● *Heel*
- ⊟ *Purl*
- ⊡ *Twisted knit*
- ⧄ *1/1 RC*
- ⧅ *1/1 LC*
- ⋊⋉ *2/2 RC*

A. Embroidered outline stitch in black over white stitches.

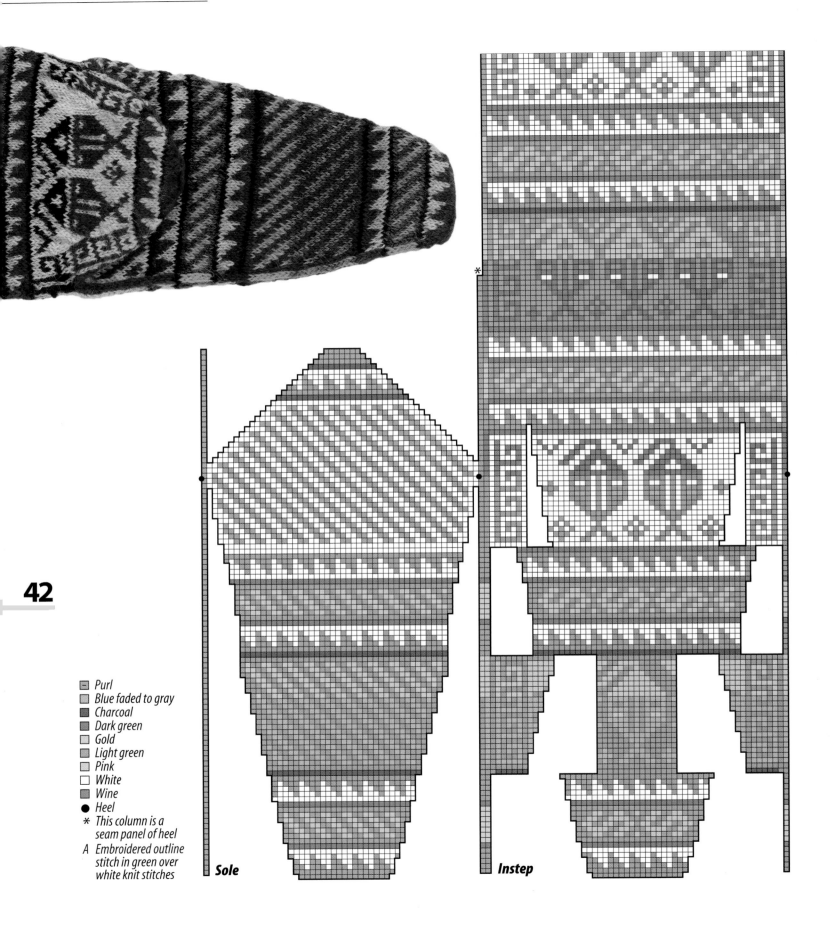

42

☐ Purl
◻ Blue faded to gray
■ Charcoal
◼ Dark green
☐ Gold
◻ Light green
◻ Pink
☐ White
◼ Wine
● Heel
∗ This column is a
   seam panel of heel
A Embroidered outline
   stitch in green over
   white knit stitches

Sole

Instep

These stockings, from Eastern Anatolia, circa 1940, are knit of 2-ply handspun wool, worked to a gauge of 10 stitches and 11 rows to the inch. They are of the highest quality, both in yarn and knitting — beautifully spun yarns, lovely colors (the original blue now faded to a silvery blue-gray), knit by the hands of a master of the craft.

The stockings were cast on at the toe using a standard *single-needle cast on* with the toe made circular by knitting through the back of the cast on stitches. (The toe has a single line of cast-on heads exposed.) Although there is no depth to the toe, it is square and the foot is tapered. Increases are skillfully hidden within the pattern, all but invisible to the eye.

Heel stitches are worked in the *waste yarn technique* because the pickup on the heel back is made in a solid color. The leg of the stocking is continued, with additional shaping in the ankle area. At the top, one round of embroidered *outline stitch* is topped with a two-color rib. Bind off is in the two colors of the ribbing. The heel is picked up from the waste yarn and decreased on every row. The blunt end of the heel is closed with a *two-stitch strap*.

Top of sock

—A

Heel back

43

15

Eastern
Anatolian
stockings

Top of sock

A synthetic yarn, much like the textured nylon of the 1950's and 1960's, was used in this pair of Turkish stockings. They are well crafted at a gauge of 9 stitches and 10 rows to the inch. The knitter used artistic license liberally (or had a highly developed sense of humor): the two stockings are clearly a pair but are not alike! (The chart is for the stocking on this page.) Whether by design or by accident, the result is thoroughly charming.

A knotted yarn button closure secures the two together when not in use. The stockings are begun with a *vertical cast on* of ten stitches. The toe is increased on every round, then the foot is worked. Instep stitches are placed on hold while a short heel flap is worked out for a *hybrid heel*. (The heel back continues the leg pattern; the heel sole is worked as charted.) After the heel is completed, the leg is continued by picking up the stitches from the instep and new stitches along the sides of the heel flap and across the top of the heel. The leg is increased at intervals with the increases hidden in pattern. When sufficient length is reached, the top is finished with a band of two-color rib. The horizontal bands of pattern between the vertical design and the ribbing are emphasized with three bands, three rows each, of embroidered *outline stitch*.

Chapter 2

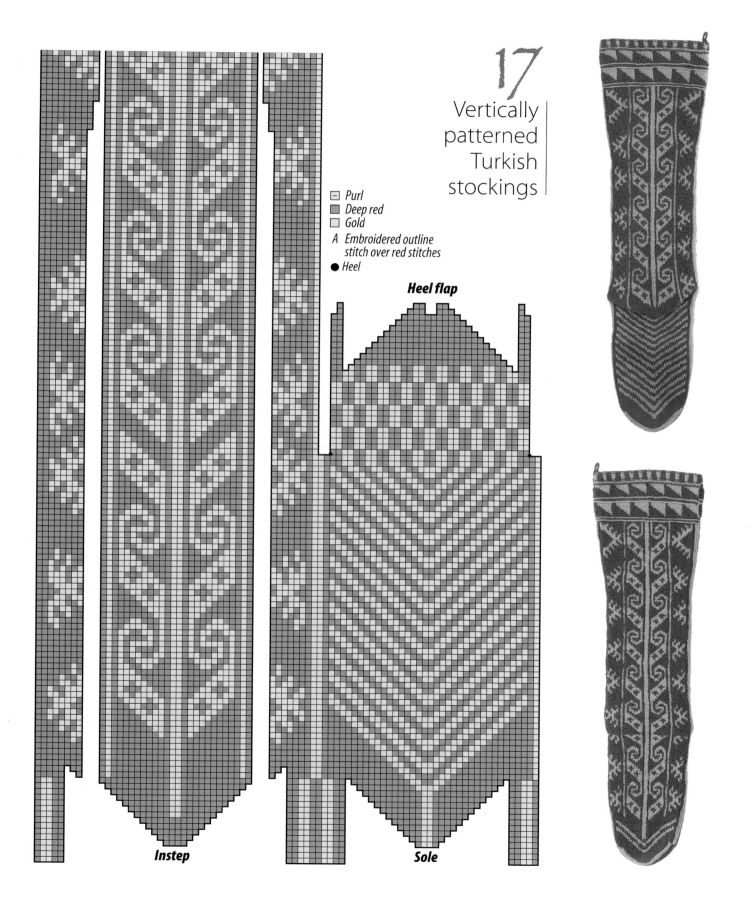

17
Vertically patterned Turkish stockings

- ⊟ Purl
- ▨ Deep red
- ☐ Gold
- A Embroidered outline stitch over red stitches
- ● Heel

Heel flap

Instep

Sole

CO 72 sts

Inc 6 sts

14x

□ Knit
− Purl
◎ Yarn over
▲ Sl2 tog-k1-p2sso
⧓ 2/2 LC

The Seres, a Slavic group in Macedonia, are the source of these wonderful socks. They are knit of handspun singles yarn. The wool used in the colored portion feels somewhat harsh, while the natural white portion is a silkier, more lustrous wool. The difference may be a result of the dyeing process.

This pair begins at the top with a cast on of 72 stitches for a 1/2 rib. After a short rib, increase to 78 stitches for 14 repeats of the cable pattern and 3 rounds of stockinette. Increase to 84 stitches and work the color pattern to the heel where the *waste yarn technique* is used for the *inserted heel*. These socks have been heavily worn and patched, therefore some details are impossible to decipher at toe and heel. The toe appears to be decreased with a balanced double decrease down to a point, but the heel is less pointed.

48

Heel back

Heel sole

18

Footed socks from Macedonia

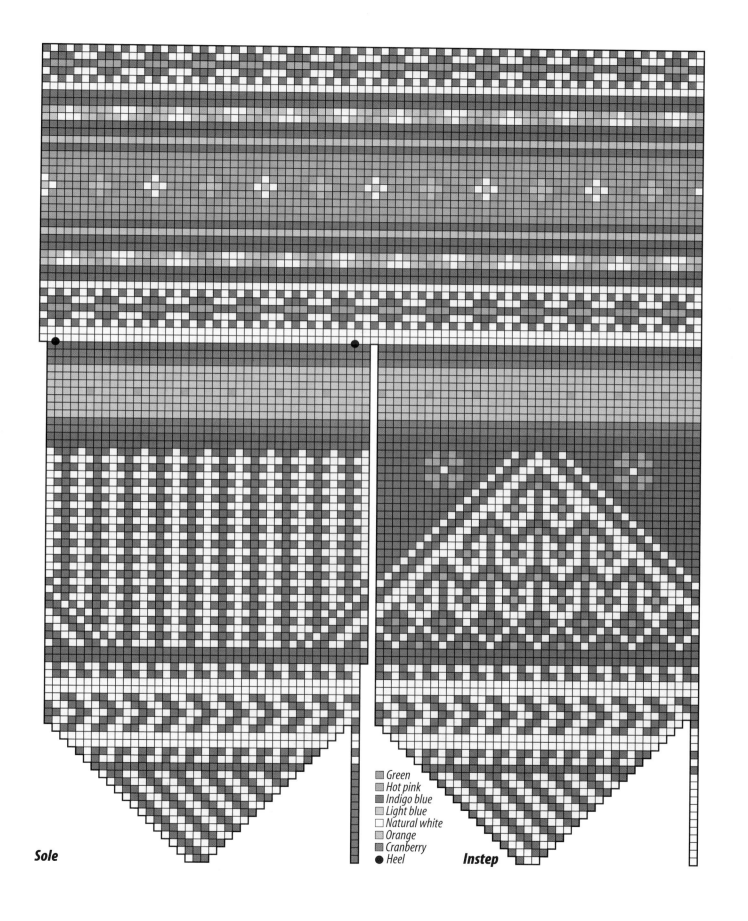

Green
Hot pink
Indigo blue
Light blue
Natural white
Orange
Cranberry
● Heel

Sole

Instep

49

19
Bulgarian point pattern with side motifs

A 2-ply handspun wool yarn in natural white wool and a slightly heavier weight yarn in contrasting colors was used for these Bulgarian women's stockings. They are worked at a gauge of 8 stitches and 10 rows to the inch.

The toe begins with an 8-stitch invisible cast on over two needles. These stitches are divided into four quarters for a *swirl toe*, initially increasing on every round, then on every third round. The floral motifs are worked in *zigzag intarsia*. When reaching the proper position for the heel, the instep stitches are placed on hold and heel back stitches are *cast on with a backward loop*. The *thumb-joint heel* is knitted with a simple vertical pattern on the back only. Instep and heel back stitches are picked up, closing the gap at the sides of the heel with a 2-stitch increase.

The leg is knitted in pattern, ending with 5 inches in stockinette above the last pattern round. The top is finished with a round of eyelets and four rounds of garter stitch. The bind off is worked as a picot: bind off 6 stitches, chain 3, repeated around. A long twisted cord for lacing through the eyelets was made from the tail turned back on itself and tied.

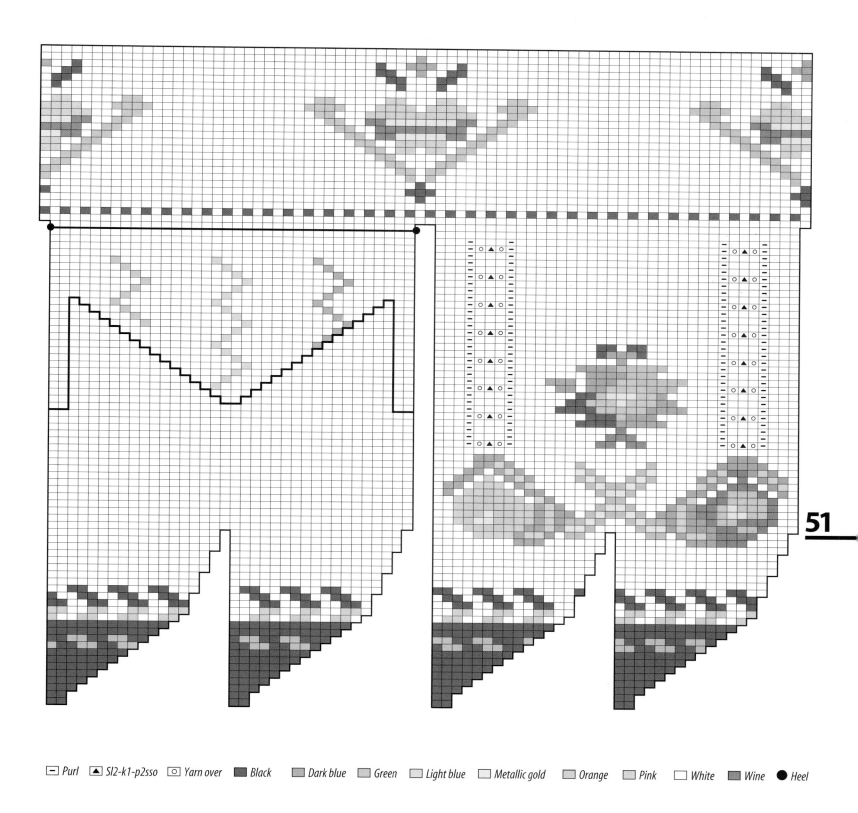

51

- Purl ▲ Sl2-k1-p2sso ⊙ Yarn over ■ Black ■ Dark blue ■ Green ■ Light blue □ Metallic gold ■ Orange ■ Pink □ White ■ Wine ● Heel

Both of these pairs of Bulgarian mens' socks were knit early in the 20th century. This pair was knit of hand-spun wool: the black a 2-ply yarn, the colors two to four strands in singles worked together. The gauge is 8 stitches and 9 rows to the inch.

The *horizontal cast on* over eight stitches at the toe is increased on every other round to the desired size, then the *color-stranded* patterns begin. The sock is knit to the appropriate length for the heel, with the *waste yarn technique* used in a solid color portion. The leg is continued to the desired length, ending with a purl round, a knit round, and bound off. The tail of the yarn is made into a short 3-ply twisted cord, knotted at the end. A *thumb joint heel* is inserted, ending with the final stitches knitted into one, the tail drawn through to close.

20
Bulgarian sock banded with stylized motifs

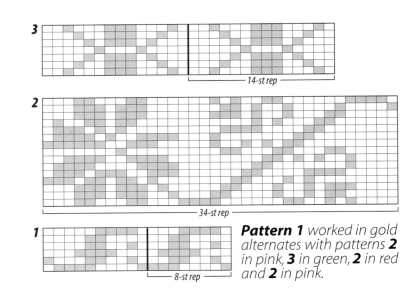

Pattern 1 worked in gold alternates with patterns 2 in pink, 3 in green, 2 in red and 2 in pink.

This Bulgarian sock with representational motifs is knit entirely of handspun cotton yarn. The yarn is not plied, instead three strands of singles are worked together and knit to a gauge of 11 stitches and 14 rows to the inch. The workmanship is such that the inside of the sock is as elegant as the outside!

It is begun at the toe with a *horizontal cast on* over twelve stitches and increased on every other round to the desired size (102 stitches). The patterns are color-stranded with floats carefully woven in on the back. The *waste yarn technique* is appropriate for the solid color heel. The leg is knit to the desired length and the stockinette finished with a single bind-off round.

The heel is inserted into the opening and several rounds worked in a narrow geometric pattern before the decreasing begins. The heel is decreased on every round, and the final few stitches are laced through and drawn together to close.

Heel pattern

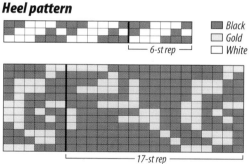

	Black
	Gold
	White

6-st rep

17-st rep

53

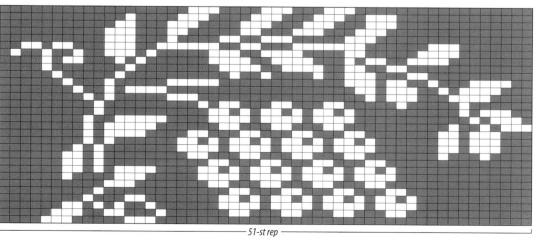

51-st rep

21
Bulgarian
sock banded with
representational
motifs

This pair of tufted toe stockings, similar to a style from the Middle East, was purchased in a small village outside of Budapest, Hungary. The work is firmly gauged at 9.5 stitches and 10 rows to the inch. The white is three strands of handspun cotton worked together while the colors are two strands of handspun wool singles worked together.

The toe is cast on around a butterfly tassel for the classic *tufted toe*. It is increased on each side of the 4-stitch side panel. The pattern begins immediately and is worked to heel depth where the heel stitches are put on hold. Since this is a small heel, it does not require half of the circumference stitches.

To return the leg to a circle, one round of *Bosnian slip stitch crochet* is worked in a contrasting color, chaining across the heel opening for a *crochet cast on*. The leg stitches are picked up through the chain head of the crochet round, decreasing the leg by four stitches, evenly spaced. The leg is continued upward in pattern, ending with a band of *Bosnian single crochet* in several colors, the final round worked as 3 slip stitches, chain 3 picot loop.

Heel back stitches are picked up through the bar on the back of the crochet chain. The work continues across the sole stitches on hold. An inserted heel is then knit outward.

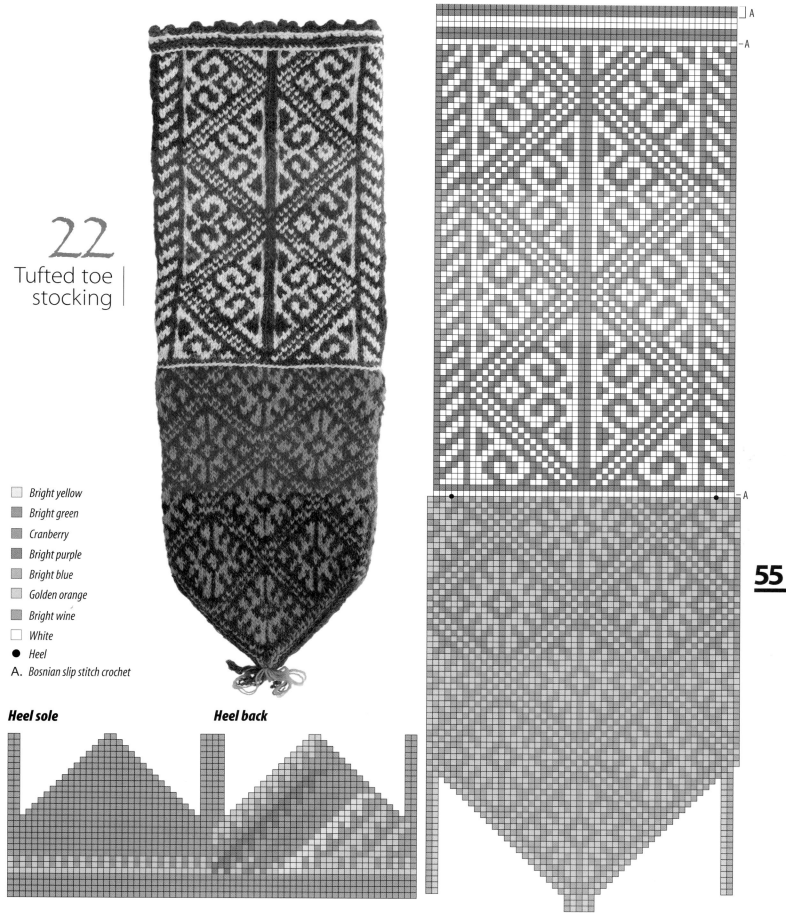

22
Tufted toe stocking

- ☐ Bright yellow
- ▨ Bright green
- ▨ Cranberry
- ▨ Bright purple
- ▨ Bright blue
- ▨ Golden orange
- ▨ Bright wine
- ☐ White
- ● Heel
- A. Bosnian slip stitch crochet

Heel sole   **Heel back**

55

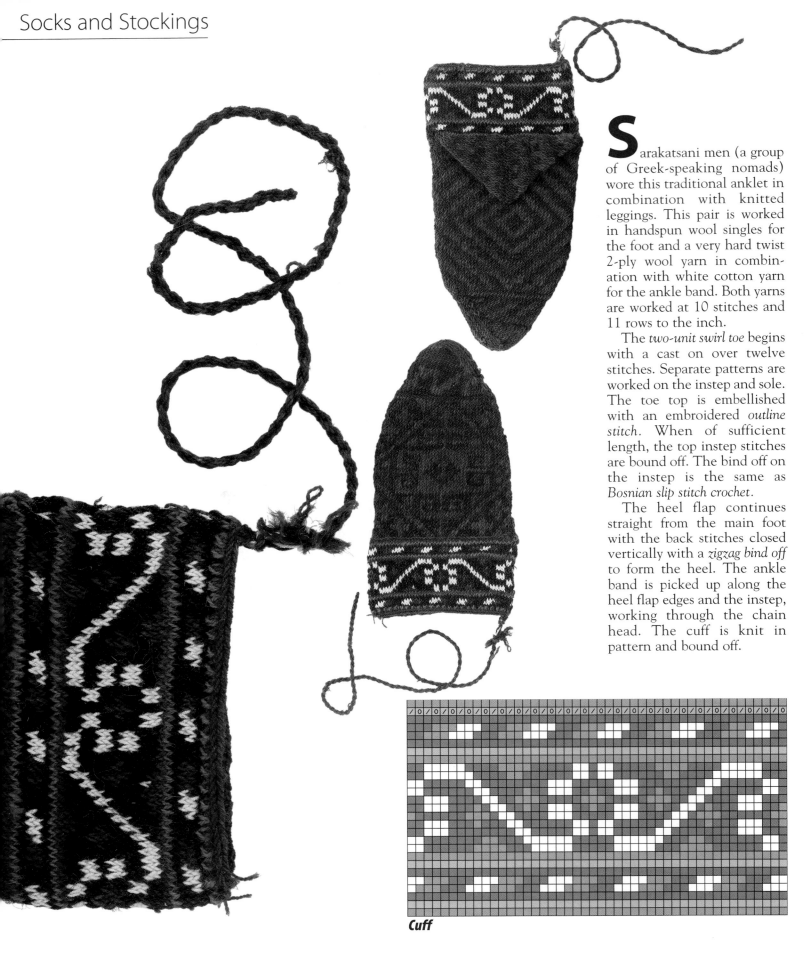

Sarakatsani men (a group of Greek-speaking nomads) wore this traditional anklet in combination with knitted leggings. This pair is worked in handspun wool singles for the foot and a very hard twist 2-ply wool yarn in combination with white cotton yarn for the ankle band. Both yarns are worked at 10 stitches and 11 rows to the inch.

The *two-unit swirl toe* begins with a cast on over twelve stitches. Separate patterns are worked on the instep and sole. The toe top is embellished with an embroidered *outline stitch*. When of sufficient length, the top instep stitches are bound off. The bind off on the instep is the same as *Bosnian slip stitch crochet*.

The heel flap continues straight from the main foot with the back stitches closed vertically with a *zigzag bind off* to form the heel. The ankle band is picked up along the heel flap edges and the instep, working through the chain head. The cuff is knit in pattern and bound off.

Cuff

Heel flap

23

Sarakatsani
anklet

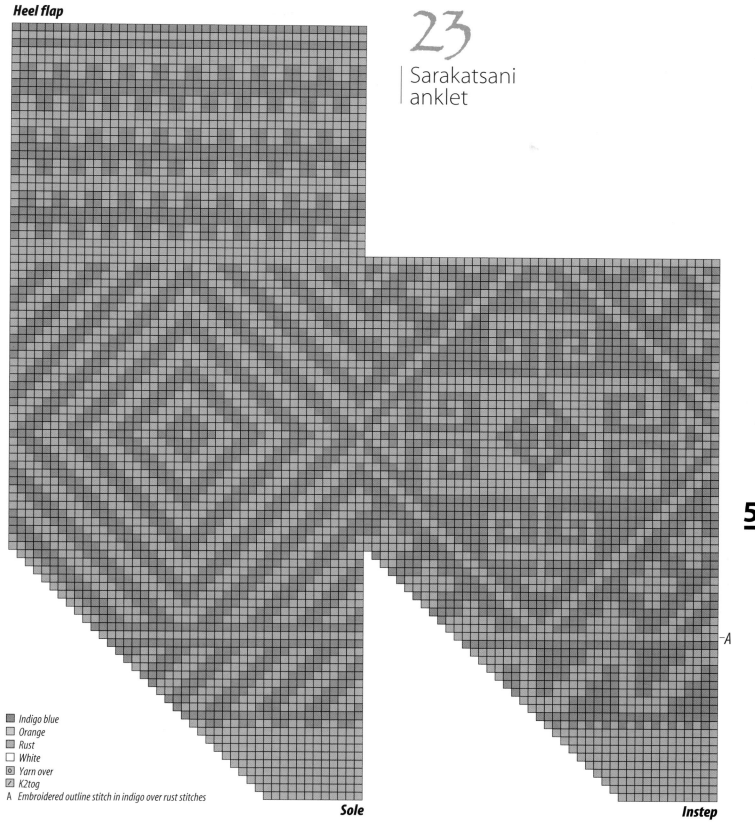

57

−A

- Indigo blue
- Orange
- Rust
- White
- Yarn over
- K2tog

A *Embroidered outline stitch in indigo over rust stitches*

Sole

Instep

24

Bulgarian
motif
stocking

Among our oldest, these Bulgarian motif stockings date to the late 1800's, or possibly early 1900's. They are knit of a plied cotton yarn with the floral motif in pink and variegated green wool. The knitting is firmly tensioned at 11 stitches and 14 rows to the inch.

Beginning at the toe, eight stitches are cast on with a *figure-8 wrap* over two needles. The toe is increased on every other round until the full width is achieved. The motif is knit on the instep prior to putting the back stitches on waste yarn for the heel (*waste yarn technique*). A half-inch above the waste yarn, the motif is worked on each side of the leg. The knitting then continues upward to the desired length and is increased to accommodate the leg. The top is finished with a round of eyelets and bound off. A twisted cord once laced through the eyelets, but only a small portion remains.

After removal of the waste yarn, the heel is worked on all stitches for one-half inch, with a small flower bud motif begun immediately. (Both heels are darned, so an accurate chart is not possible.) The heel is then decreased on every round.

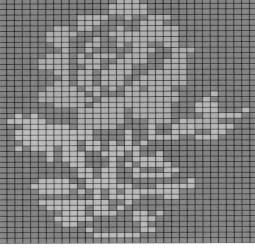

■ *Black*
□ *Pink*
□ *Green*

These little socks are from the area formerly known as Yugoslavia. They are worked to a gauge of 7 stitches and 9 rows to the inch in a cabled synthetic yarn in blue, a plied synthetic yarn in light blue, and an unspun synthetic fiber in the red accent.

The sock begins with a 10-stitch cast on over two needles. These stitches are worked in one direction to create a *rectangular flap* twelve rows deep. To close the toe and begin circular knitting, eleven stitches are picked up along one side of the rectangle, the initial ten stitches of the cast on are worked, and eleven stitches picked up along the remaining side, thus creating a round. The main motif is on the instep with a chevron pattern on the sole.

At the heel, the instep stitches are knit onto *waste yarn*. Heel back stitches are cast on with a *backward loop cast on*; the heel then continues, first straight, then decreased. After the heel stitches are bound off, the heel is turned inside out and the two bound off edges are bound off together. With the heel finished, the stitches on the waste yarn are picked up for the leg. This is worked in a 1/1 striped ribbing that ends in a purl round and then is bound off.

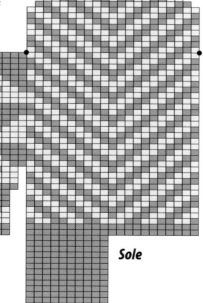

Instep

Sole

Heel

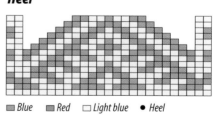

■ Blue ■ Red □ Light blue • Heel

25
Child's
sock

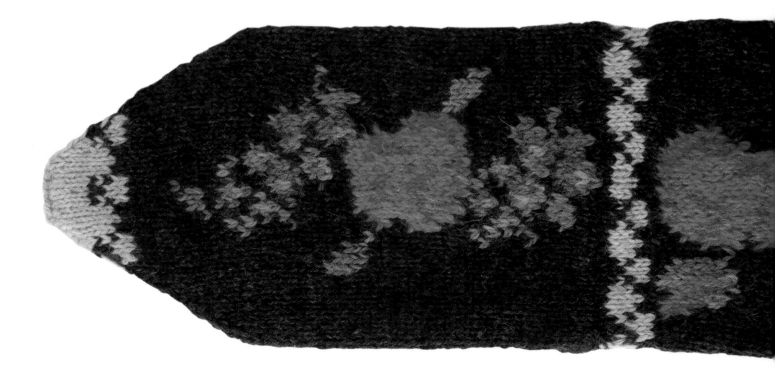

26
Bulgarian floral motif

Unlike the older stockings, these Bulgarian stockings, circa 1990, are cast on at the top. The pair is knit in a soft 2-ply commercial wool yarn at 7.5 stitches and 10 rows to the inch. After one round of eyelets, the leg is worked down to the toe, inserting *waste yarn* for the heel and binding off at the toe. The floral pattern is worked in *zigzag intarsia*, resulting in a padded appearance. The leg pattern is worked on both the front and back.

The heel, worked in the traditional manner, is inserted into the leg/sole upon the removal of waste yarn stitches. The final stitches are bound off together to match the toe.

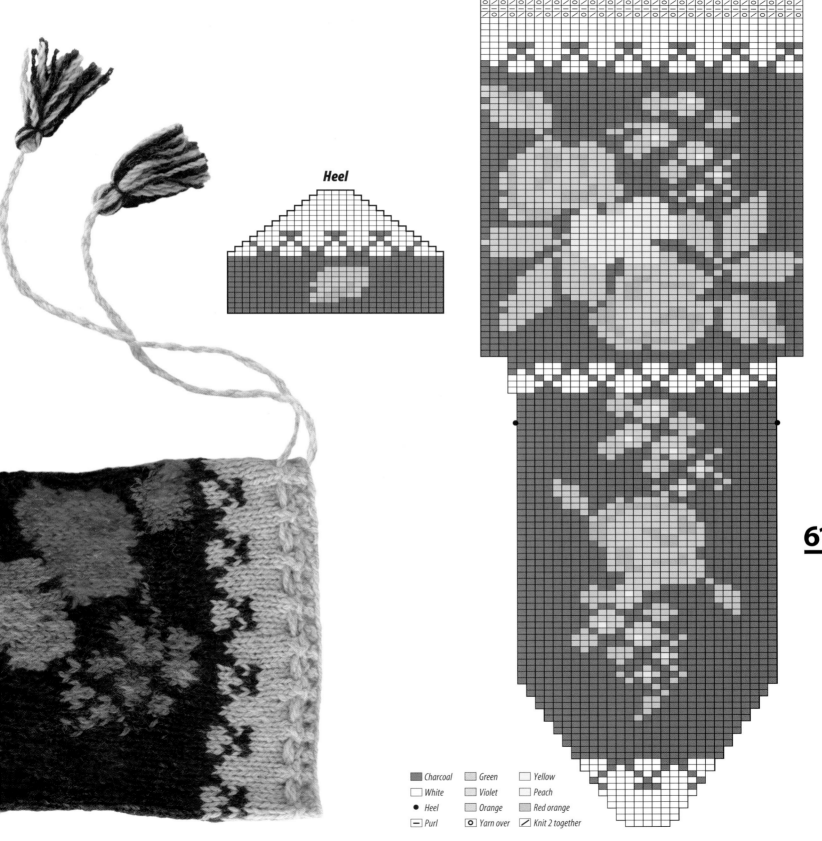

Heel

Charcoal | Green | Yellow
White | Violet | Peach
● Heel | Orange | Red orange
— Purl | ⊙ Yarn over | ⟋ Knit 2 together

61

From thumb to thumb-joint: The heel of most Eastern socks is inserted after the leg is knitted, much as a thumb is added to a mitten. The opening for the heel can be made in several ways; an ingenious example is the crochet cast on used on this tufted toe sock (pp. 54-55). A thumb-joint heel provides an easy fit.

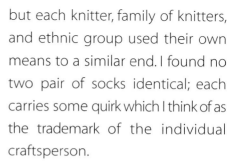

Construction Techniques

The socks and stockings under consideration here are a true folk art, a craft handed down through the generations by a generally illiterate people. Each generation learned from the hands of an earlier generation.

Without the assistance of formal documentation to standardize the techniques, a wide diversity developed. Each knitter adapted a technique to suit an individual working style, yet stayed true to the overall concept. To the casual eye, the work of the various groups may appear the same, but each knitter, family of knitters, and ethnic group used their own means to a similar end. I found no two pair of socks identical; each carries some quirk which I think of as the trademark of the individual craftsperson.

But, for the sake of documentation, generalization is required. Various categories are established for each basic style beginning with the cast on for the toe, working upward through several toe shapes and various heel options, and ending when the leg is of appropriate length.

How to's:

1
Figure-8 wrap cast on

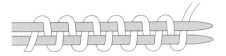

a. With two needles held side by side, tail yarn at left, wrap yarn in a figure 8, ending with an equal number of stitches on top and bottom needles.

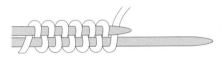

b. Snug yarn securely around needles. When ready to knit, slide bottom needle tip out beyond wraps in order to allow top stitches to be moved to working needle without losing any bottom needle stitches. Working close to top needle tip, knit across. When all stitches have been completed, take tail over working yarn to secure last top stitch.

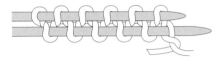

c. Rotate needles to bring bottom needle into position to knit. Knit through back of loop for a standard stitch or through front of loop for a twisted stitch.

Tools of the trade

A set of five double pointed knitting needles is the requisite tool. The ideal would be to have needles pointed at one end and hooked at the other. Since such are not commercially available, today's knitter will have to resort to the occasional use of a crochet hook as an auxiliary tool. The yarns vary from fine to medium weight, and needles ranging from 2mm through 3¼mm (American size 0-3) of a fairly short length are usually appropriate.

The stitches are divided evenly on four needles with a fifth working needle. In cases where a center front/center back stitch is required for design, the first and third needles will each carry one additional stitch. Since the socks have a front and back rather than two sides, the rounds begin and end at the side rather than the center back. The most meticulous knitters position the round change to occur on the inside of the leg where any jog in design is least visible. (This does establish a left and right sock.) With vertical design development, the jog is often camouflaged; it is readily apparent only in horizontal bands.

Casting on

Traditionally, the socks and stockings of this region are cast on at the toe. In a few instances, primarily in some areas of the Balkans, they begin at the top and work to the toe where the stitches can be grafted or bound off together (probably a modern 'westernization' of technique).

Casting on at the toe may be done by wrapping the yarn on two needles for an invisible cast on or in a number of decorative ways, including a tufted circular cast on, a backward loop-tubular cast on, and a backward loop mount with visible ridges. The stitches are established in a circular mode (even though, in some cases, the actual knitting may begin flat, working off in opposite directions, before commencing with circular knitting).

1
For a *figure-8 wrap cast on*, hold two needles side by side in the left hand. Beginning at the left with a short tail in the front, take yarn behind and over top needle, then behind and under bottom needle. Continue this process until the necessary stitches have been mounted, half on the top needle and half on the bottom needle, ending with the yarn coming around the bottom needle and out to the back (1a). These stitches are now ready to be knitted, working across the top needle first (1b). At the end of the first needle, the tail should be taken down and over the working yarn to secure the last stitch worked on the top needle. Then, the needles are rotated to bring the bottom needle into position for knitting (1c). If the stitches are knit in the front of the loop, those on the second needle will be twisted. When this cast on is placed horizontally for a *flat toe*, these stitches are commonly twisted to tighten. Although visible when viewed directly, this twisted row disappears into the

fold of the toe. When the cast on is placed vertically for a *vertical cast on with toe depth*, the stitches on the second needle are usually worked through the back loop to eliminate the twist. Without the twist, these stitches are looser than subsequent stitches.

2 For a *straight wrap cast on*, hold two needles side by side in left hand. Beginning at the left with a short tail in the front, take the yarn behind and then over the top needle, wrapping counterclockwise around the two needles, ending with the yarn going under the bottom needle and coming out to the front (2a). With the yarn held in place around the bottom needle, the top stitches are then knit (2b). At the end of this row, the tail yarn should be securely wrapped around working yarn or the end stitch is easily lost. The needles are rotated (2c), and the stitches now in the top position are knit. With this wrap, all stitches on both needles are in a standard mount (with leading side of loop in front of needle). But, even more important, the needles are not encircled individually as with the figure-8 cast on; therefore, the tension is the same as that of the standard knit stitch worked on the same needles.

Some socks have a rectangle that encircles the point of the toe. This rectangle provides *toe depth* and is established by positioning the cast on vertically.

The work progresses circularly. In order to create a rectangle, allow yarn to travel loosely along edges.

3 Alternatively, an initial rectangle can be worked flat by leaving a longer tail (about 15") at the beginning of the cast on. After the cast on, the stitches on the top needle are worked with the ball yarn by knitting one row, purling one row, knitting one row. The ball yarn is dropped and the same process repeated on the other needle with the tail yarn, working two rows. The tail yarn is dropped and knitting begun in the round. It is possible to work the rectangle in only one direction, but when working in opposite directions from a cast on, the stitches are always off by one-half stitch at each end. This one-half stitch jog at the cast on wrap is less noticeable when the cast on is centered.

4 Some socks, specifically those of the Lurs of Iran, have a simple knit-purl textured pattern in the toe depth/side seam panels that originate with the cast on stitches. The pattern is developed on every other row with alternate rows of knit stitches. Other socks may have a color-stranded pattern in the toe depth/side panels. They can both require a central row. If they do, one row must be knit across one needle of the initial straight wrap cast on. Henceforth, the end of this row is the beginning of each round. Patterning must begin on this first complete round, the first needle of the round holding the second half of the initial wrapped stitches.

2 *Straight wrap cast on*

a. With tail coming to front between needles, wrap around both needles in counterclockwise direction, ending with ball yarn coming out to front between the needles.

b. Slide bottom needle out to right to prevent wraps from dropping off needle tip as top stitches are worked. The wraps should be snugged securely on needles. Working close to top needle tip, knit across. Take tail yarn down and around working yarn to secure last stitch.

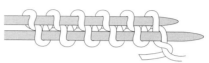

c. Rotate needles to bring bottom needle into position to knit. Stitches on both needles are in a standard mount.

3 *Working in two directions*

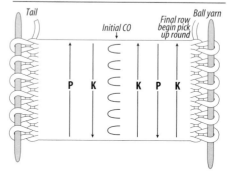

Illustration of working out in two directions from center wrap cast on, working to the right with ball yarn and to the left with tail yarn.

4 *Textured pattern in toe depth*

A textured pattern in the toe depth panel begins with an initial row. (1). Illustration shows knit rounds alternating with p2, k2, p2 rounds.

65

5 Two-color cast on

a. Begin straight wrap with tail at back, yarn coming forward between needles. Take yarn under bottom needle, wrapping two needles in counterclockwise direction. End with yarn coming over top needle, then between needles to back.

b. Repeat with second color, tail over yarn of first color. Wrap as before.

c. Dropping second color, bring first color yarn over second, wrap as before. At end of first needle, secure last wrap with other color yarn. Knit wraps as with one color, maintaining proper color sequence.

6 Backward loop cast on

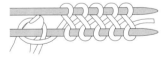

a. Mount stitches alternately on two needles. Loops are mounted with leading side of loop on front of needle in standard mount.

b. When all stitches have been mounted, rotate work. Ball yarn will now be in position to knit. Cast on ridge lies between two needles. Knit across top needle, working through back loop of stitches. Rotate needles to bring second needle into position to knit. Again, knit back loops.

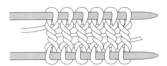

c. Ridge and round of twisted stitches will make a three-ridge section of horizontal lines between standard knit stitches of toe.

5 Some socks with the cast on vertically positioned for toe depth are worked in two, sometimes three, colors. The toe depth stitches become decorative side panels encircling the foot and branching up the leg. As the work progresses outward from the cast on at the center front of the toe, the colors will be off by one-half stitch (just as in grafting). This is not readily visible as long as there are at least two stitches in each color and the cast on is centered.

This variation of the straight wrap is most suitable for a *two-color cast on*: with tail at back, bring yarn between two needles, down and around to back, up and over and around both needles to back again, up and over and between two needles to the back (5a). To change color, lay new yarn over yarn to be dropped. (When first learning, it may be helpful to tie the two yarns together with an overhand knot before beginning cast on.) Take new yarn up and between two needles and wrap as before (5b). Drop second color, then lay first color over yarn dropped. Repeat wrap (5c). When all stitches have been wrapped on the two needles, take second color yarn around last yarn used, thus securing the last loop.

Maintaining color sequence, knit across the top stitches. Rotate needles clockwise and knit, twisting yarns at edge to secure as before. Continue in this manner, working four to six rounds between the two needles, maintaining color pattern as established on chart.

As in the one-color cast on, the initial rectangle can be worked flat, maintaining the proper color sequence, if desired.

6 The *backward loop cast on* is the simplest method. It can be worked on one or two needles.

It is interesting to note that many Western knitters mount their stitches with the bar leaning up and to the right. Whereas the Eastern knitter prefers the opposite, mounting their stitches with the bar leaning up and to the left. The Eastern way results in a standard stitch mount, a decided advantage when casting on with backward loops for the heel pickup.

For a cast on with two needles, the needles are held side by side in the right hand, cast on a stitch, first on one needle, then the other needle (6a). Each loop must be drawn onto the needles snugly. Continue alternating in this manner until the required number of stitches has been mounted. Then turn work over, ball yarn is now to the right. There will be a row of slanted bars from the cast on facing upward (6b). Knit through the back loop of the stitches on the upper needle. Rotate the needles and knit through the back loop of the stitches on the second needle, now in the upper position. Henceforth, all stitches will be knit in the standard manner. This cast on results in a 3-ridge section that is very flexible (6c). It is usually used with a *two-unit swirl toe* where this flexibility allows the sock to conform to the contour of the toes.

7 The *circular cast on*, in my opinion, is the most difficult cast on. Whereas all the preceding cast on techniques can be used interchangeably with a number of toe styles, the circular cast on is used exclusively for the tufted toe, a pointed style.

The first step is to create the tuft. Even if the body of the sock is worked with plied yarns, this toe is usually worked in singles. A tuft of singles has more character since the twist causes the strands to swirl together; plied yarns tend to be limp. The tuft is formed by wrapping a small butterfly around the thumb and forefinger (or two fingers, which I find more comfortable) with two strands of singles (7a). The cast on is most often done in two colors, wrapping first one color and then the second color in the butterfly even though both could be wrapped simultaneously. (When first attempting this cast on, I suggest using a plied yarn in only one color.) Each color is wrapped three or four times so that, when folded over, the tuft will have three or four double loops plus three to four inch tails. After wrapping, the butterfly is slipped off (7b), then folded at the figure eight crossover. The yarn to the ball is coming out from the crossover. A tail is wrapped through the circle at the crossover and secured to the ball yarn (7c). A tail yarn is then securely wrapped around the fold and tied to create a tassel (7d), the tail is then looped around the tuft but not tied. This loop forms a circular wrap around the tuft

through which the stitches of the toe are picked up.

The initial round is worked with a crochet hook. Grasping the tuft, with tail and ball yarn at base of tuft, go under the strands of the encircling loop with crochet hook and draw up a loop from the ball (7e), then another loop through the first (draw up a loop, chain one in the vernacular of crochet; 7f, g) for each stitch. This process is repeated nine more times for a total of ten stitches.

The loops can be transferred to a knitting needle, either one loop at a time or when all loops have been formed. (Working with a hooked knitting needle made this technique straightforward: the loops remained on the needle.) To better visualize the top and sole, I pick up the first five loops and transfer them to a knitting needle, then repeat the sequence and place these loops on a second knitting needle. The tail yarn is then snugged securely into place, drawing the stitches together as tightly as possible. When excess tail yarn is cut, the cast on is complete.

8 This cast on is normally worked in two colors and the stitches are arranged as follows: begin at the middle of the four side panel stitches across top (or bottom) stitches to the four stitches of the next side panel, ending with two side panel stitches. The color sequence for the pickup would be: A, B, A, B, A, A, B, A, B, A. Once the stitches have been arranged in this manner,

7 Circular cast on for tufted toe

a. Wrapping butterfly over two fingers (two strands of singles should be used; a single strand is shown for simplification).

b. Remove butterfly from fingers.

c. Fold butterfly, take tail through circle, and secure.

d. Wrap fold with tail and tie to make tassel.

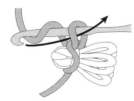

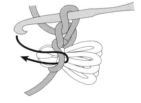

e. Wrap loop around tuft, draw up loop with crochet hook.

f. Chain one.

g. First stitch on crochet hook is now complete. Repeat process of drawing up a loop, chain one until ten stitches have been completed.

8 Circular cast on in two colors

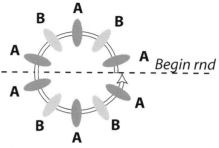

After drawing up five stitch loops in color sequence, they are placed on first needle for half of toe. The process is repeated, and the remaining stitches placed on second needle for second half of toe.

9 Single-needle cast on

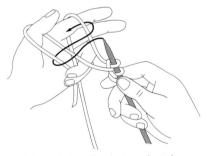

a. Make a slipknot for the initial stitch, at a distance from the end of the yarn (about 1-1/2" for each stitch to be cast on). Arrange both ends of yarn in LH as shown. Bring needle under front strand of thumb loop, up over front strand of index loop, catching it ...

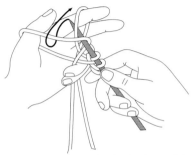

b. ... and bringing it under the front of the thumb loop. Slip thumb out of loop, and use it to adjust tension on the new stitch. One stitch cast on.

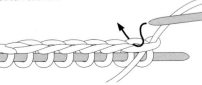

c. After casting on, rotate needle, bringing yarn into position to knit. Cast on will appear as chain stitches on top of needle.

10 Knit in the stitch below

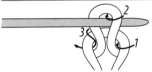

Knit into the stitch in the row below before (1) or after (3) knitting the stitch (2) for an invisible increase.

one or two rounds can be knit to make a short knoblike protrusion at the tip of the toe or increasing can begin to shape the toe.

A 2-3 loop tuft is sometimes used as the start for a *4-unit swirl toe*. The tuft is usually limp, having been formed with a plied yarn.

This type of cast on is obviously not designed for an enclosed shoe. But omitting the tuft and proceeding directly to picking up the stitches around the loop will make a suitable circular cast on for enclosed shoes.

9 Single-needle cast on:

beginning with a loose slipknot, mount 15-18 stitches on one needle with a standard long tail cast on. At the end of this initial cast on, do not turn the work. Instead, rotate the needle clockwise, bringing the cast on edge up to the top. The cast on edge looks like the chain heads of a bound off edge. Working through the middle of the chain head, pick up and knit an equal number of stitches opposite the initial cast on stitches. With this many stitches, it is easier to pick up and knit half of the stitches on a second needle, the remainder on a third needle. Since there is no chain head for the final stitch, this stitch must be picked up through the initial slipknot stitch. This final pickup is often more easily drawn through with a crochet hook, then transferred to the knitting needle. Divide the initial cast on stitches on the first needle evenly onto two needles. This cast on is used for a *square toe*.

Increasing

There are two methods commonly used to increase the toe stitches to fit the foot: (1) pick up and knit and (2) make one. The shape of the toe is often the determining factor as to which of the two is preferred.

Pick up and knit is associated with the vertical positioning of the cast on for a toe with depth, the angular positioning for a swirl toe, and the circular cast on for the tufted toe. To work this increase, the needle tip enters the end of a row (which may be only one stitch deep at the point of pickup), the tip is wrapped in the standard manner, the loop then drawn through to the front. If the end stitch is firm and tidy, the pickup can be worked around half of the end stitch, the needle entering in the middle of the stitch. The pickup can be worked around the entire end stitch, with the needle entering between the first and second stitches of the row, but this makes a bulky ridge while eliminating an entire edge stitch.

10 A *knit in the stitch below* increase is sometimes practiced by Eastern knitters. Its use is normally limited to adjusting the number of stitches for pattern purposes on the top or sole of the toe. It is worked as the name implies, by knitting in the stitch below (1), then knitting the stitch on the left needle (2) for a

right slant. Or, for a left slant, by knitting a stitch (2), then with right needle tip, entering the left side of the loop of the stitch below to knit a second stitch (3).

11 *Make one* is usually associated with the cast on positioned horizontally for a flat toe. A make one increase can be achieved in three ways, the end result being the same. Most Western knitters use *make one raised*, lifting and twisting the bar between two stitches. The bar is raised and knit on the same row.

12 Some prefer the *make one, backward loop* between two stitches. The backward loop is mounted on one row and knit on the following row. Whichever method is preferred, these increases must be made directionally, pairing a slant to the right with a slant to the left.

13 Eastern knitters, especially in the Balkans where the flat toe with a horizontal cast on is common, prefer to do a *make one, yarn over*. Again these must be made directionally for a proper taper, one slanting right and one slanting left. On one row, the increase is anticipated with a yarn over; on the following row, the yarn over is worked. To avoid a hole, the yarn over must be worked twisted. For a right-slanting increase, the yarn over should come from the back over the top of the needle; it is knitted through the

front loop to twist the stitch on the next row. For a left-slanting increase, the yarn over comes to the front under the needle then over the needle to the back; it is knitted through the back loop to twist the stitch on the next row.

I find this Eastern method far superior. The *make one raised* makes for a tight stitch, breaking the rhythm of the knitting on that row only. The *make one, backward loop* gives a more even tension, but breaks the rhythm of the knitting on two rows. The tension on the *make one, yarn over* is even and the rhythm of the knitting is never broken.

When pairing the left- and right-slanting make one increases, the line of increases becomes more distinct when the increases lean away from the seam. When the paired increases lean into the seam, the increase line is less distinct. Either can be used as long as it is used consistently. The direction of the new stitch will be the same as the angle of the yarn on the front of the needle in the first step of the make one increase.

11 *Make one raised*

(Arrows show path needle takes when knitting.)

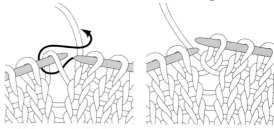

a. Make one raised, left.

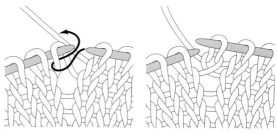

b. Make one raised, right.

12 *Make one, backward loop*

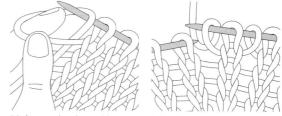

Make one, backward loop, LEFT. Paired increase, RIGHT.

13 *Make one, yarn over*

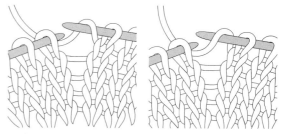

Make one, yarn over, left slant, LEFT. Make one, yarn over, right slant, RIGHT.

69

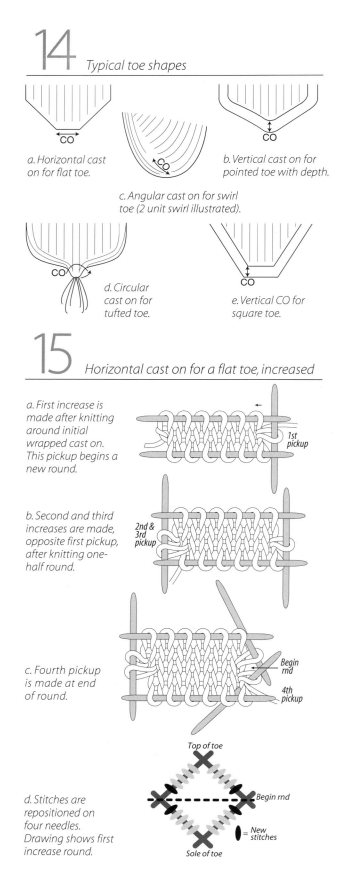

14 *Typical toe shapes*

a. Horizontal cast on for flat toe.

b. Vertical cast on for pointed toe with depth.

c. Angular cast on for swirl toe (2 unit swirl illustrated).

d. Circular cast on for tufted toe.

e. Vertical CO for square toe.

15 *Horizontal cast on for a flat toe, increased*

a. First increase is made after knitting around initial wrapped cast on. This pickup begins a new round.

1st pickup

b. Second and third increases are made, opposite first pickup, after knitting one-half round.

2nd & 3rd pickup

c. Fourth pickup is made at end of round.

Begin rnd

4th pickup

d. Stitches are repositioned on four needles. Drawing shows first increase round.

Top of toe

Begin rnd

= New stitches

Sole of toe

Toe shapes

14 There are five basic toe shapes, and after cast on, stitches are arranged differently for each: (a) horizontal cast on for a flat toe, (b) vertical cast on for a pointed toe with depth, (c) angular cast on for a swirl toe, (d) circular cast on for a tufted toe, and (e) vertical cast on for a square toe with depth. In every case, the cast on makes the first round of the knitting.

15 Arranging the cast on horizontally results in the flat toe shape preferred among many of the ethnic groups in the Balkans. The toe is flat at the tip, the width of the tip depending upon personal preference. This toe can be cast on by either the *figure-8* or the *straight wrap* methods; for even tension on the figure-8, work the stitches of the second needle twisted.

Regardless of which method is used, the shaping proceeds in the same manner. First, the stitches are wrapped over the two needles, the wraps then knitted off both needles. At the beginning of the next round, using a third needle, pick up and knit one stitch between the two cast on needles (15a). Knit across the first needle. With another needle, pick up and knit two stitches between the two cast on needles (15b). Work across the second cast on needle. With the fifth needle, pick up and knit one stitch to end the round (15c). At this time, reposition the stitches on the

needles, placing half of the initial cast on stitches on what was the first needle with the first picked up stitch and the remaining half with the second picked up stitch on a second needle. Then, divide the other stitches likewise, the third picked up stitch and half of the stitches on what was the second needle on a third needle, the remaining half with the last picked up stitch on the fourth needle (15d). The horizontal toe is then increased on every other round. If using the *make one raised*, knit one round even. On the next round, begin increasing. If using the *make one, yarn over* or *make one, backward loop*, begin the sequence on the initial round, knitting the new stitches on the following round. Continue increasing until sufficient stitches have been added to fit the circumference of the foot.

16 Arranging the cast on vertically creates the toe shape preferred by most of the ethnic groups in the Middle East: the toe with depth (14b or e). It can begin with either the *straight wrap* or the *figure-8 wrap*. If using the latter, the stitch mount on the second needle should be knit through the back loop to eliminate the row of twisted stitches.

This style of toe can be used to create a tapered toe by working a four to six row *rectangular flap* before picking up two or three top and bottom stitches. Or, with a longer rectangle, it can be used for a blunt toe, thus enabling more stitches to be picked up along the edge. For the tapered toe, working circularly on the initial round is most typical. For the blunt toe, the rectangle is usually worked flat, out in one direction with the tail yarn and in the opposite direction with the ball yarn. Working in this manner keeps the cast on in the center, thus centering the one-half stitch jog mentioned earlier. This is particularly important when working in two colors or when the toe depth/side panels are worked in knit-purl textured patterning. Textured pattern is usually worked on every other row. Knit the first row after the cast on at center front, and begin the texture on the next round (illustrations 3 and 4, p.65).

The actual pickup can be worked around half of the stitch across half of the rectangle and around the entire stitch on the other half to keep the line of pickup consistent across the end. Or, the pickup can be around either half or all of the edge stitch (as discussed earlier), jogging at the center to keep the stitch width of the rectangle consistent from end to end. The latter is preferred, especially when the side panel is worked in pattern.

17 After the stitches are picked up on both top and bottom, the stitches can be repositioned, from center side panel to center top on the first needle, center top to center side panel on second needle, likewise across the bottom (17a). Or, the side panels can

remain on separate needles with top and bottom needles (17b). In part, how one sets up the stitches on the needles depends upon how one visualizes the pattern: as units with a top, two sides, and bottom or as four quarters. In either case, the round always begins at the center side panel. I prefer to set the stitches up in quarters when the top and bottom each have a mirror image pattern and into units when there is one central pattern for the top and bottom. It may be easier to shape the toe with two side panels in combination with a top and bottom setup, then reposition the stitches if desired for the foot.

Once the stitches have been positioned as desired, begin increasing for the foot. In most cases, the pick-up-and-knit increasing continues as established on each side of the top and bottom on every round, especially if the initial pickup was only two or three stitches. With the blunt toe, the increase may occur on every other round.

For the swirl toe, the cast on is usually positioned at an angle. The swirl toe can begin with the *figure-8 wrap, straight wrap*, or *backward loop cast on*, and some four-unit swirls begin circularly with *a tufted toe*. Increasing usually begins immediately after the initial round of knitting. The toe can be divided into two halves or into four quarters, use of halves being the more common. In either case, the increase is worked by the pick-up-and-knit method.

16 *Vertical cast on for toe depth, pickup*

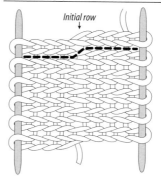

Initial row

Jogging the pickup at the initial cast on row at center of rectangle maintains complete stitches across width of rectangle, an important consideration when multiple colors are used in the panel. If edges are snug and tidy, pick up through middle of the edge stitches. This is especially important for the tufted toe where four stitches in two colors make up the side panel. If the whole stitch is encircled, the second color is not visible. Illustration has dotted line running one full stitch into rectangle for clarity.

17 *Repositioning stitches for vertical cast on*

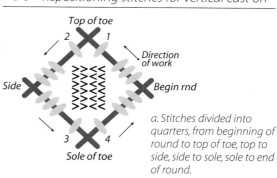

Top of toe
2 1
Direction of work
Side
Begin rnd
3 4
Sole of toe

a. Stitches divided into quarters, from beginning of round to top of toe, top to side, side to sole, sole to end of round.

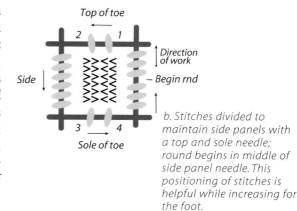

Top of toe
2 1
Direction of work
Side
Begin rnd
3 4
Sole of toe

b. Stitches divided to maintain side panels with a top and sole needle; round begins in middle of side panel needle. This positioning of stitches is helpful while increasing for the foot.

71

18 Increasing swirl toe

a. Division of stitches for a two-unit swirl. Increases are made at the end of second and fourth needles on every round.

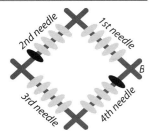

b. Division of stitches for a four-unit swirl. Increases are made at end (or beginning) of every other round for a tapered toe with increases on every round in same position for a rounded, blunt toe. A four-unit swirl does not need to be paired with the opposite swirl.

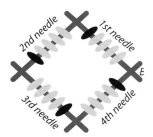

19 Increasing tufted toe

a. Stitches are on two needles after cast on round.

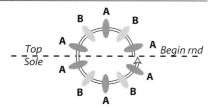

b. Traditional position of stitches on needles. The center top and sole stitches are respectively on first and third needles. If two stitches are required at top and sole, the increase would be made by knitting in stitch below, the new stitches mounted on second and fourth needle.

c. Alternative positioning of stitches on needles.

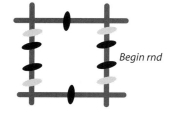

The pickup occurs at the beginning of the angular section for a slant up and to the left, at the end of the angular section for a slant up and to the right. At the point of pickup, the round will be only one stitch deep. Shaping is seldom reversed for the second sock: the angle of the swirl is usually the same for both socks.

18

If the swirl is in two units, the first and third needles hold the initial cast on stitches. The increase occurs on the edge between these two needles, at the end (or beginning for opposite slant) of the second and fourth needles on every round (18a). The stitches on these two needles will be the new picked up stitches. The stitches can be repositioned as the work progresses to more equally divide the numbers as long as the pickup is maintained as established.

When the swirl is composed of four units, the initial cast on stitches are divided equally on four needles. The increase occurs at the beginning (or end for opposite slant) of each needle (18b) on every other round for a tapered toe or on every round for a rounded, blunt toe.

19

The tufted toe is cast on by one method, the *circular cast on*, the only variation being whether or not an additional round or two are knit prior to increasing. When there are four side panel stitches on each side of the toe, plus one top and bottom

stitch, the preferred method for increasing is to pick up and knit the new stitches at each end of the side panels.

The traditional setup of stitches is to divide the side panel stitch at the center point, between two stitches of the same color (19b). The stitches flanking the center stitches are of a contrast color; before knitting the final contrast color of the four side panel stitches, the working yarn is drawn snugly across the back of the center two, thus creating a ridge. If an even number of stitches is required for the pattern, an increase at the center top and bottom stitch can be made on the next round. This increase is usually made by *knitting in the stitch below*. Since this is a pointed toe, the increases are worked on every round.

An alternative setup of the stitches might be easier to work during the increase section of the toe: establish the stitches on the needles for four side panel stitches, one top stitch, four side panel stitches, one bottom stitch (19c). If set up in this manner, the round begins in the middle of the first four-stitch side panel. If set up in this manner, the two centermost side panel stitches tend to stay flat, not round up into the characteristic ridge of the traditional socks.

A four-unit swirl toe, as described in the preceding section, may begin with a tuft. In this case, the initial stitches are divided on four needles with the increases made at the end (or beginning) of every other round.

20 The *tubular strip for a square toe* begins with three (or more) backward loop stitches that are then knit as a tube, usually in two colors. First, make one backward loop with the main color, then with the contrast color, ending with the main color. Since there is only one stitch in the contrast color, this center stitch will be loose with the yarn lying across the needle. The first knit row will secure this stitch. On the first round, do not turn the work. Bring the main color yarn across the back from left to right and knit the first stitch from the other end of the needle. Do not snug the yarn tight across the back; this strip is not a cording. Bring the contrast color from under the main color to twist the yarns and knit the middle stitch. Again, bring the main color from under the contrast color to twist and knit the final stitch in main color. Continue in this manner until a tubular strip of 15-18 rows has been worked. This strip will lie horizontally across the front of the toe.

The strip is dangling from one needle. Rotate this needle clockwise and, with a second needle, pick up one stitch at the end of each row of the strip, working through the middle of the edge stitches with the main color yarn. Rotate the work clockwise to pick up and knit across the initial backward loop stitches. With a third needle, knit through the first cast on stitch in the main color. With a new

contrast color strand (i.e., the contrast color is not carried around), knit the contrast color stitch. Drop the contrast color and knit the main color stitch. With a fourth needle, use the main color to pick up and knit through the middle of the stitch at the other end of every row of the strip.

The stitches can then be repositioned on the needles, dividing at each side just before (or after) the contrast color stitch and at the center top of the toe and center bottom of the toe. The tapered toe/foot is usually increased on every 4th to 6th round from the tip of the toe to the heel division. How often the increase occurs depends on the length and width of sock necessary: the greater the width, the closer the increase spacing; the longer the length, the farther the increase spacing. The increases may occur on each side of the initial three-stitch toe strip which continues up the foot as a decorative side panel. Or the increases occur within the pattern, subtly positioned so as to be invisible. The contrast color stitch can be worked as established on every round, or this stitch can be put on hold and chained up between the two edge stitches with a crochet hook when the knitting is finished.

The square toe can also begin with the *single needle cast on*. For a single stitch side panel, one stitch is picked up and knit at each side between the initial cast on stitches. For a two-stitch side panel, the initial stitch is

20 *Tubular strip for a square toe*

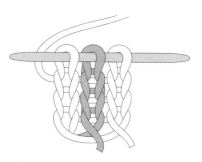

The tubular strip for the square to begins with a backward loop cast on, most often in two colors.

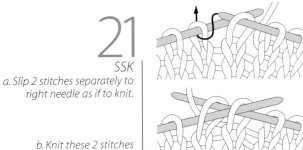

21

SSK
a. Slip 2 stitches separately to right needle as if to knit.

b. Knit these 2 stitches together by slipping left needle into them from left to right.

22

Maintaining color sequence
a. Back sole stitches placed on hold, cast on with backward loops then close circle.

b. When heel back stitches are picked up through the backward loop cast on, the color pattern knit stitch is inverted.

Leg

Sole

Leg

Heel back

23

Beginning the inserted heel
To close gap, two extra stitches can be picked up at each side. On the next round, both stitches are decreased. By slanting the decreases into one another, the maneuver becomes invisible.

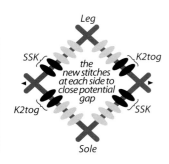

Leg

SSK

K2tog

the new stitches at each side to close potential gap

K2tog

SSK

Sole

24

Two inserted heel shapes
a. Thumb-joint heel.

Leg
Heel
Pick-up line

Leg
Heel
Pick-up line

b. Straight decrease heel.

picked up at the beginning of the round at one side, the top (or bottom) stitches knitted to the other side where two stitches are picked up and knitted, the bottom (or top) stitches knitted to the first side with the round ending with the final pick up and knit stitch. The two-stitch side panel is more typical. The spacing of the taper of the toe/foot is the same as the preceding sock.

Decreasing

The decreases used are the same as those used traditionally by Western knitters: knit 2 together for a right slant and slip 1 as to knit, knit 1, pass the slipped stitch over for a left slant. The latter has largely been replaced by American knitters with the SSK.

21 To work an SSK, slip one stitch as to knit, slip the next stitch as to knit, pass the left needle tip back through the front of the two stitches just slipped and knit them off together.

As with increases, when the decreases slant away from the seam, the line of decreasing will be more outstanding. When the decreases slant into the seam, the line will be less visible.

Heel styles

There are two basic styles of heels: inserted and flap heels, plus a hybrid of the two. And, each style can take various shapes.

The *inserted heel* is the style most commonly known to Western knitters; it has been adopted by many Western

sock knitters as a simplified method for turning the heel. An obvious advantage with this heel is the ease with which it can be replaced since none of the heel stitches is an integral part of the instep stitches. But it also offers greater potential for patterning. When working the inserted heel on an Eastern sock, the foot is worked, some means provided for opening the sole/back leg stitches, the leg is worked, and then the heel is inserted. (In the case of Western knitters, the direction is reversed.)

There are several ways that the back stitches can be opened. In Eastern Europe, where vertical patterning is not common, the opening can be established in two ways. The first requires the use of *waste yarn*. The stitches to be opened are first knit with a waste yarn, then these waste yarn stitches are re-knit with the sock yarn. After the leg is completed, the loops of the stitches above and below the waste yarn are laced onto two needles by picking up the leading loop of each stitch. This is an easy process if a finer needle is used for this initial pickup of the loops. The waste yarn is then removed and the stitches worked outward for the heel — more or less as a toe in reverse.

Or, using a long blunt needle (sold as a weaver's needle or bodkin) threaded with waste yarn, the sole stitches can be removed, lacing thru the loops from left to right in a method called *auxiliary needle technique*. The threaded needle can then be laid (right to left) beside one of the knitting needles just freed of stitches. The knitting needle will be on top, the weaver's needle in the lower position. The new leg stitches are then cast on with a *straight wrap* using the working yarn, wrapping around the threaded weaver's needle and the knitting needle. Bringing yarn from back to front between the two needles, the yarn is wrapped counterclockwise as many times as necessary to replace the leg stitches. The yarn will end, coming around the lower needle, then between the needles to the back. After wrapping the needles to cast on the back leg stitches, the front leg stitches are knit. When reaching the back leg, the wrapped cast on stitches are worked off the knitting needle, letting the lower stitches slide off the weaver's needle onto the waste yarn. This method eliminates the need to pick out the stitches knitted with waste yarn, but it is a more tricky maneuver.

Some Western knitters use another method for this type of heel. In this case, the sock is knitted as a long tube, the back leg stitches clipped at center back in the proper location and picked out to each side. Eastern knitters do not use this method since an entire row of knit stitches is removed.

Moving eastward, where vertical patterning is common, waste yarn techniques are not appropriate if the pattern is to be continuous in the heel back and leg. Any waste yarn technique will be off by one-half stitch when the stitches are worked in the opposite direction giving a visible jog in vertical patterns whether colored or textured. To camouflage the jog, some knitters work a round or two in a solid color on the leg portion just above the heel opening, thus breaking pattern continuity. The sole stitches do not require a break since the direction of knitting on the heel is a continuation of the sole proper. As long as the pattern is broken on the heel back, the waste yarn technique is suitable. But, as a general rule, whenever two or more yarns are in use in each round, whether of the same color or contrast colors, waste yarn methods are not recommended.

22 In order to maintain vertical color pattern, the most common method is to put the sole stitches which continue into the heel on hold (22a). The back leg stitches are cast on with backward loops, maintaining the proper color sequence. This cast on is less visible if formed with the bar leaning up and to the left (Eastern style); if leaning up and to the right (Western style), the stitches appear twisted when picked up and worked outward for the heel. When the heel is worked, the heel back stitches are picked up through the backward loop stitches. The 'V' of the stitches will be inverted in the heel back when compared to the back leg, but the color alignment of the pattern will be true (22b).

23 When picking up the heel stitches, gaps occur at each side of the heel, depending on how tightly the knitting has been gauged and the method used to provide the opening. Usually one or two extra stitches are picked up on each side and removed in the next round or two, thus eliminating any potential problem. Occasionally, the extra stitches are retained as side panel stitches between the decreases when shaping the heel.

I recommend picking up two stitches and removing them side by side on the next round (with the decreases leaning together to become invisible) unless the design of the heel requires them as side panel stitches.

Once the heel stitches have been placed on four needles, the heel must be shaped. There are two basic methods:

24 (a) *thumb-joint heel* or (b) *straight decrease heel*. The former gets its name from the method used to measure its shape. The heel is worked outward in a straight line, using all heel stitches with no decreases, to a depth equal to the first thumb joint of the wearer of the sock. When this depth is reached, decreasing begins on every round. The second, a straight decrease heel shape, is decreased on every round, beginning after the stitches are picked up, making a very shallow heel. The extra depth of the thumb joint heel allows it to follow the contours of the foot more naturally.

In either case, four stitches are decreased each round, and the decreases are paired: use a k2tog decrease for the right slant and a sl1-k1-psso (or SSK) for the left slant. If there are no side panels, the decreases are usually placed side by side. If side panels are integral to the design, the panel stitches are usually maintained in the heel with the decreases positioned at each side of them.

25 Whether a thumb-joint or a straight decrease heel, the heel is finished similarly. With no side panels, the heel might go out to a point where the last few stitches are laced through and drawn together (25a) or they might be ended with a blunt straight line. In the latter case, the remaining stitches from the heel sole and heel back could be bound off together or grafted (becoming a horizontal join, 25b). On occasion, all the stitches are bound off, then the heel back and sole are bound off together (wrong sides together) by working through the middle of the already bound off stitches from back to front: a hooked needle simplifies this process.

Where panels are maintained, decreasing usually continues until all stitches are removed except the panels. These often are laced

through and drawn together or grafted (forming a vertical join, 25c). An interesting closing for the heel seen on occasion, both with side panels and without, is a *crochet rosette*. The rosette is created by working decreasing rounds in *Bosnian slip stitch crochet* (explained in Chapter 4). This treatment is both unique and quite elegant (25e).

Another interesting closing for the heel is sometimes used in conjunction with the tubular strip cast on. In this case, the heel is 'squared' over the base by working a *strap* across the final stitches. (25d). The strap is usually two or three stitches wide, matching the panel at the sides. With the heel back stitches on one needle, the sole stitches on another, and the side panel stitches on needles at opposite ends, the side panel stitches at one end become the strap stitches and are worked as a row. At the end of each row, one side stitch is joined with one back/sole stitch until all stitches have been removed from the heel back and sole needles. The working procedure is to slip the first stitch of each knit row, joining the last stitch of the row with a heel back/sole stitch with an SSK. Turning the work, slip the first stitch of the row, ending by joining the last stitch with a heel back (or sole) stitch with a purl 2 together. The final two or three strap stitches are then grafted with the side panel stitches at the far end.

In some groups in Eastern Europe, what appears to be an inserted heel is not always inserted. Instead, the heel is worked immediately after the completion of the main part of the foot, prior to knitting the leg. In this case the instep stitches are placed on hold while the heel is knitted. When vertical patterning is involved on the back of the heel/leg, the sole stitches are continued into the heel with stitches cast on with backward loops for the heel back. Otherwise, the instep stitches can be knit onto a waste yarn, these waste yarn stitches then knit in the sock yarn and continued into the heel. Or, the instep stitches can be put on hold with an invisible cast on for the back heel stitches. The heel is worked outward to completion, as before. When the heel is finished, the stitches from the instep are placed on the needles with stitches across the heel back picked up for the leg. Where the gap would occur between heel back and sole, two new stitches are picked up on each side. These stitches increase the circumference of the leg for a looser fit.

26 Another method, seen further east, is based on a single round of crochet worked in a contrast color. After working across the sole heel stitches, the front leg stitches are bound off in a contrast color. When reaching the sole heel

stitches, an equal number of chain crochet stitches is worked above, thus opening the heel (26a). The last chain is joined into the front leg bind off. To complete the leg, pick up and knit new stitches, working only through the back side of the chain loop (26b). The front side of the chain loop creates a decorative contrasting horizontal line around the ankle. Place the sole heel stitches on the needles, the back leg heel stitches are picked up through the bar behind the line of chain loops, thus retaining one-half of the chain loops in a continuous circle around the ankle (26c). The heel is worked outward to a slightly greater length than the usual thumb joint measure, then decreased on every round as on previous heels. An interesting aspect of this particular heel is the use of fewer than half of the circumference stitches: the heel is usually offset on each side by two or three stitches. The stitches picked up to close the gap at the sides are retained as part of the heel. This heel is most often seen in conjunction with the tufted toe. (This heel can also be inserted before completing the leg if desired.)

27
The *flap heel* is based on a knitted flap extending the sole of the sock. This heel type takes three forms: (1) gathered flap, (2) joined flap, and (3) strapped flap.

The *gathered flap* is found in Bosnia, Albania, and the Black Sea region of Turkey. Although there are exceptions, this heel is most often used in conjunction with a swirl toe and a leg with *Bosnian crochet*. This style of stocking is almost boot-like in appearance, especially where any quantity of Bosnian crochet is involved. Bosnian crochet, being very inelastic, almost rigid, allows little ease so the instep/ankle section must be large enough to accommodate the passage of the wearer's heel. Therefore, the sock is commonly increased on the upper side of the instep (not on the sole). In some cases, the Bosnian crochet encircles the leg, making a continuous band. In others, the Bosnian crochet is only used on a portion of the leg immediately above the heel flap with the portion above the instep continuing in knit stitches.

For this heel (27a), the foot is knitted to the leg front depth at which time the instep stitches are placed on hold while the sole stitches are knit flat to the length appropriate for the heel. This must be sufficient to allow the flap to cup up and around the heel. At this point the stitches are rapidly decreased, the decreases incorporated into a band of one or more rounds of Bosnian crochet that begins the leg portion of the sock. This round thus includes picking up stitches along the edge of the heel flap. Starting at the middle of the inside edge of the leg, stitches are picked up and bound off (i.e., worked as slip stitch crochet) along

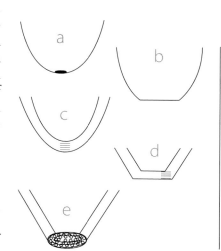

25
Heel termination
a. Laced stitches form a point.
b. Grafted or bound off together stitches form a blunt, horizontal line.
c. Side panel stitches extended into heel and grafted vertically form an unbroken side panel around foot.
d. A strap worked across the final stitches forms a square heel.
e. Bosnian slip stitch crochet forms a rosette.

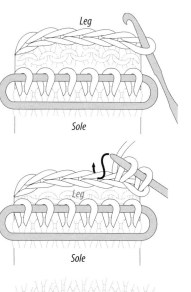

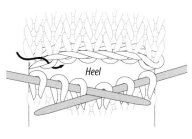

26
Crochet CO at heel
a. Front leg stitches are worked as slip stitch crochet (i.e. bound off), then heel stitches are put on hold with crochet chain above to close circle for leg.

b. On next round, new stitches for the leg are picked up and knit through only the back of the chain head.

c. When picking up stitches to knit heel, the new stitches are picked up through the bar behind the chain head. Thus, a continuous horizontal line made of the front of the chain head encircles the leg.

77

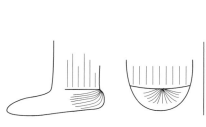

27
Flap heel variations
a. Gathered heel, side and back view.

the edge of the heel flap. Upon reaching the heel flap stitches, the simplest way to gather the heel is to decrease with a k3tog and bind off on this initial round of the Bosnian crochet. But, the resulting heel is fairly wide and does not cup the heel nicely. Another way is to decrease over three rows beginning with k2tog across, then p2tog across. These decrease stitches are worked in alternate stitches of the colors used in the sole pattern. The final row of k2tog is incorporated into the pick up and bind off round as before.

A third method makes use of short rows. The heel flap is knit to about two-thirds of the length required. At this point, the knitting continues as established, working one less stitch at each end of every row until about one-third to one-half of the stitches remain between the angling edges (slip first stitch and don't work last stitch). The yarn is then broken off. The pick up/bind off sequence of the Bosnian slip stitch crochet begins at the center of the inside of the leg as before, picking up along the edge of the heel flap. Upon reaching the end stitches of the angled short row section, the bind off continues as established. The stitches of the heel back are then gathered with a k2tog across as a part of the bind off for this round of Bosnian crochet. In some cases, even the angular edges are gathered. This method allows the continuation of the sole pattern throughout the shaping. And, a better cupping of the heel is achieved with the shaped edges

culminating in a short section of gathering at center back. Its success depends upon keeping the end stitches tight in the short row section.

27b
Joined heel flap: Among the Greek-speaking nomads of the region, the heel flap is extended to the desired length (sufficient for the sides of the flap to meet at the center back of the heel) and then bound off together, on either the inside or outside of the sock.

An interesting bind off for this heel is a *zigzag bind off*, a decorative element that is less bulky than the typical bind off together method. The flap stitches are knit to the halfway point. With half of stitches on each of two needles and working yarn at center, the flap is folded with wrong sides together. With a third needle, knit first stitch beyond fold on second needle (side holding stitches which were not worked). Then purl one from first needle. Pass first stitch worked over last stitch worked. Repeat these steps: knit 1 on second needle, pass over, purl 1 on first needle, pass over, until all stitches have been removed. Upon completion, there will be a zigzagging chain up the center back of the heel flap.

When the heel is complete, new stitches are picked up along the edge, worked across the instep and along the second edge. A short cuff-like leg is worked, creating a socklet that is worn with leggings. In a few cases, the cuff-

like section is worked separately and sewn into place on the foot.

27c
The *strapped heel* is much like a Western style turned heel in reverse. Whereas the Western square heel is worked downward with the flap, then worked back and forth for the base, the Eastern version has the flap as the base and a strap as the heel back. To work this heel, a few center back stitches are worked back and forth, joining the last stitch of the section with a stitch from the side section. With knit side facing, the stitches are joined with an SSK decrease; with purl side facing, the stitches are joined with a p2tog decrease. When all stitches from the two side sections have been removed in this manner, the strap stitches are usually bound off. Leg stitches are then picked up along the heel flap edges, beginning at the center of the leg, and across the strap (picking up around the entire chain head of the bind off). Knitting is then resumed in the round.

28
The *hybrid heel* combines the flap and inserted heel. The advantage of this heel is greater ease in pulling the sock on over the heel of the wearer; it fits much like a thumb joint heel. When the instep depth is completed, those stitches are placed on hold while the sole is extended with a short flap. When the flap is of sufficient

the center of the inside leg, knitting across the instep, picking up along the other side of the heel flap, then casting on above the stitches on hold to put the leg back into the round. When the leg is completed, a short inserted heel completes the sock.

Leg

As stated earlier, the leg of Eastern socks and stockings has a front and back rather than two sides. The ankle is rather loosely fitted and no shaping is required for the socks. In some cases, two to four stitches may be added to the circumference of the leg just above the inserted heel position. This allows for easier passage of the foot through the leg of the sock while the foot of the sock can be fitted more snugly. Stockings, being of longer length, require increasing to accommodate the calf. While Western stockings neatly line the shaping up the center back, making a seam that becomes a focal point, Eastern stockings are shaped within the pattern at both sides, the increases subtly positioned so as to become invisible.

When the leg length is sufficient, the top of the stocking may be finished in a number of ways, only a few of which include either the popular Western ribbing or cuff. The simplest method is to bind off the top and allow it to curl. A more decorative *double stitch bind off*, one that helps to counter the inclination to roll, is usually worked in two colors. With last round knit in alternate colors, the first three

stitches are knit in established colors. All stitches of this round must be knit loosely since they become the bound off edge. The first stitch is passed over the next two stitches on the right needle. A new stitch is knit, the first stitch on the right needle passed over the two subsequent stitches. The bind off continues in this manner until all stitches have been removed. Double up on the pass overs on the last two stitches since there is no third stitch.

Another decorative treatment to finish the leg is a round of eyelets. Sometimes closely spaced, other times widely spaced, the eyelets are topped with a knit round and bound off. When eyelets are included, a long twisted cord is usually made from the tail yarns. The cord laces through the eyelets to serve as a decorative garter. Some tops have a few rounds of garter stitch, others have a band of *twisted purl* or *Bosnian crochet*. When the edge treatment is complete, the ends are either tied off and allowed to hang free or made into a long twisted cord for tying around the sock or stocking (supposedly to hold the sock in place, but of equal importance as a decorative element).

A Western knitter would carefully work all ends in at this point, whereas many Eastern knitters have tied on any new colors and consider this sufficient finishing. Only among the Balkan knitters and those of Asiatic Russia is finishing the inside considered necessary; much Bulgarian work is as neat on the inside as on the outside.

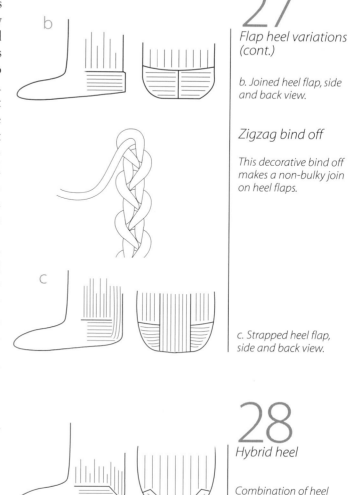

27
Flap heel variations (cont.)

b. Joined heel flap, side and back view.

Zigzag bind off

This decorative bind off makes a non-bulky join on heel flaps.

c. Strapped heel flap, side and back view.

28
Hybrid heel

Combination of heel flap and inserted heel.

Color patterns can be worked in different stitches — all in the same piece.
In this Black Sea stocking (pp. 38-39), ABOVE, FROM BOTTOM TO TOP, single crochet and slip stitch
(both worked Bosnian-style: in the back loop only) combine with Eastern crossed stitch knitting.

Design Techniques

The construction of socks is almost inseparable from their design, but in this chapter we will emphasize techniques and methods of working that contribute primarily to the design (in the sense of patterning and decoration).

Many of these design techniques deal with the use of lots of color in circular knitting. Often color-stranded designs use more than two colors in a round, many times with long carries. In other cases, intarsia motifs are worked — in the round. Crochet is often used in color pattern, sometimes

in the same round as knitting. The Eastern preference in crochet (working in the back loop only: Bosnian crochet) forms tidy horizontal ridges of color that can only be mimicked by embroidery.

Texture provides relief in Eastern socks—in both senses. Discover several ways to work traveling stitches (here, untwisted knit stitches cross each other on a stockinette ground). Two-end knitting is used, both for added thickness and decoration.

Clearly this full bag of tricks can translate to almost any knitted piece.

How to's

1

Unsecured floats

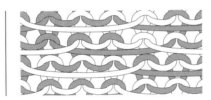

2

Securing left float with right yarn
Raise yarn in left hand enabling right-hand yarn to cross left yarn. Keep left yarn up for at least two stitches, then lower so that right yarn crosses left once more.

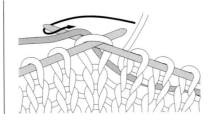

3

Securing right float with left yarn
After entering stitch, wrap right-hand yarn around tip of needle. Wrap left-hand yarn for new stitch and...

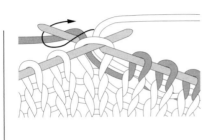

82

...take floating yarn back into position before drawing new stitch loop through old stitch.

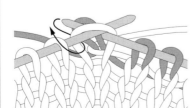

Stitch division

Eastern socks and stockings are worked with sets of five needles, the stitches evenly divided on four needles with a fifth working needle. Normally, this division of stitches occurs at each side and center front/center back. Then, if an odd number is required for a single center front and center back stitch, the 1st and 3rd or 2nd and 4th needles each carry that additional stitch. In most cases, after the cast on and setup of the toe, the new round starts at the side. Usually, this is practical since the design is easily 'read' in four sections, especially if there is no vertical side seam pattern. When there is a side seam pattern, the repeat is often more readily visualized with the side seam stitches on separate needles, especially when establishing the pattern. When working an intarsia motif, shift stitches to accommodate all motif stitches on one needle if feasible.

Color-stranding techniques

The use of many colors is common throughout this region of the world. Tensioning the yarn around the neck and working on the purl side in the traditional manner greatly simplified the use of multiple colors. This old technique has been largely abandoned in favor of 'modern' Western technique.

Short of resurrecting the old Eastern method, there is not one simple solution to the problem of managing multiple color carries. I will outline

methods which might prove helpful. These techniques should be tried and adapted to suit personal working styles.

1
Two colors is simple. I carry the dominant color in the right hand, the other color in the left hand. The stitches are then knit according to pattern from either the right or left hand, allowing the yarn not in use to float freely across the back of the work. As long as the floats are no greater than 1", there is no need to secure them.

2
But many of the designs from this region require long floats. If the dominant color is in the right hand, it is easy to secure the floating left-hand yarn. Simply lift the left finger to raise the floating yarn and cross with the working yarn to work the next stitch. When the left floating yarn is lowered, the working yarn will cross and secure it again. Rather than lower the yarn immediately after the stitch is completed, I work at least one more stitch to prevent the floating yarn from being secured under both sides of one knit stitch. This would produce too much bulk for the stitch to absorb without bulging and allowing the floating color to peek through.

3
Securing the floats with only the right-hand yarn is sometimes sufficient. But, with many of the designs in the socks and stockings under consideration, long floats can

occur in the yarns carried in each hand. Therefore, the ability to secure a floating right-hand yarn is also important. After entering the stitch, some knitters like to wrap the floating right yarn around the tip of the needle, wrap the left yarn for the new stitch and take the floating yarn back into position before drawing the loop through the stitch. This is simple, but my objection to this method as typically practiced is, again, the floating yarn is secured behind both sides of the new stitch. If worked on two successive stitches, it is a good technique, especially when working on the short double point needles used for socks.

4 Another technique is to loop the right-hand floating yarn to the left around the next few stitches on the left needle. Knit these stitches with the left yarn. To release the loop, draw right needle tip under the front after completing the stitch in process. This secures the floating yarn behind the stitches, thus eliminating the bulge and unwanted color exposure. Many find they have more control of the tension on the floats with this technique, especially on larger pieces.

If one prefers to carry both colors in one hand, whether left or right, twisting the yarns will secure the floats. It has often been stated that twisting the yarns when changing colors will eliminate holes in the knitting. This is not necessary; in color stranding, holes will not appear at color changes since there is always a stranding yarn to hold the work together. But twisting the yarns to secure a float is an important skill. I like to carry the yarns, one on each side of the forefinger, controlling the yarns respectively from the top of the finger by lifting or the underside of the finger by scooping. When twisting is necessary in the middle of a long float, the positions of the two yarns are reversed. If the yarns are reversed alternately, top to bottom and then bottom to top, the two balls do not become entangled.

5 For me, carrying multiple colors requires the combination of the two-hand carry and the twisting technique. This makes a three-color carry easy. When using four colors, I carry the two most used colors in my right hand, one on each side of the forefinger, and the other two in my left hand, again tensioned on each side of the forefinger. This allows me to secure floats with both the twist and crossover technique. Granted, this takes some practice, but if each technique is first mastered alone, the combination of the two just takes patience and practice. Although not totally a tangle-free procedure, order can be maintained even in complex designs. Also, when colors are used in only a small area, they need not be carried throughout; they can be worked with *zigzag* or *motif intarsia* techniques.

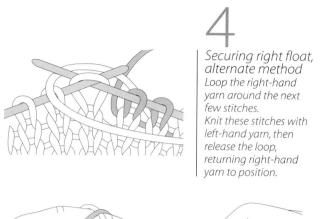

4
Securing right float, alternate method
Loop the right-hand yarn around the next few stitches.
Knit these stitches with left-hand yarn, then release the loop, returning right-hand yarn to position.

5
Multiple color carry
One method of carrying two yarns in each hand. In most designs, any additional colors are used only in small sections and therefore not carried throughout.

6

Interlocking motif yarn, right

To interlock along right edge while working color-stranded row, enter last background stitch. Take right needle tip behind motif yarn and draw it to the right. The background yarn will cross over to secure the motif yarn.

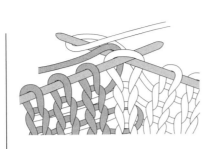

7

Interlocking motif yarn, left

To interlock along left edge while working 2-step row, knit background stitches while slipping motif stitches. Knit one stitch beyond motif. Enter next stitch. Take motif yarn to left over right needle tip. Background yarn will cross over motif yarn. The motif stitches are then worked left to right while slipping background stitches just worked.

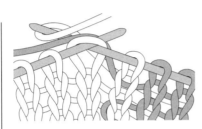

84

Motif knitting

Many knitters believe that intarsia type motifs require flat knitting. Not so! In Bulgaria, the practice of working such motifs in the round has long been common. Some of the motifs can be quite complex, but most incorporate some background stitches within the design. While learning, position all the motif stitches on one needle, plus one background stitch on the right side and two background stitches on the left side.

On the initial round of the motif, the pattern is color-stranded from right to left, as usual (*color-stranded row*). At the end of the motif, the pattern color is dropped while the knitting continues around in the main color. When reaching the motif on the next round (pattern color now at the left end), the stitches on the motif needle to be worked in the main color are knit while slipping the contrast (pattern) color stitches as if to purl. The main color yarn, now on the left side of the motif needle, is dropped. *Working from left to right*, the pattern color yarn is picked up, coming up and over (crossing) the main color yarn. All main color (background) stitches just worked are slipped purl-wise while the pattern stitches are worked (*two-step row*). These may be purled or *knit in reverse*, the latter eliminating the need to turn the work. The pattern yarn is now on the right, where it is dropped for use in the next round. Slip any remaining background stitches on the right end to the motif needle. Return to left end of

motif needle to complete round in main color. On the following color-stranded round, the contrast color is picked up, coming over the main color.

6

To insure smooth edges to the motif, yarns can be interlocked prior to changing color for the motif. Along the right edge of the motif, interlock on the color-stranded row in the last stitch before the color change of the previous round or the round in progress, wherever the color change first occurs. To interlock, take right needle tip behind contrast color yarn before knitting last stitch in main color.

7

Along the left edge of the motif, the interlock can be worked two stitches beyond the color change. If the color change moves to the left, the yarn can be carried out and interlocked on either the color-stranded row or the two-step row. If the color change moves to the right, the yarn should be interlocked at the end of the motif on the color-stranded row. To interlock, take right needle tip under contrast color yarn held in left hand before knitting last stitch; then knit motif in reverse (or purl). Or, always interlock in the first stitch after the motif by first entering the stitch to be worked and wrapping the needle tip with the motif yarn then wrapping the main color yarn. The motif yarn is then taken back into position before drawing new loop through stitch. Both techniques are the same as those used in securing floating yarns when color stranding. Interlocking as described will control distortion of the first and last stitch of a color block by securing the contrast color prior to the color change.

This technique requires that on alternate rows the motif stitches are worked from right to left, color-stranding the pattern in the traditional manner. The rows between are worked in two steps. The first step is to knit the background from right to left; the second step is to knit (or purl) the contrasting pattern stitches from left to right. Thus the ability to knit in reverse greatly simplifies this process. This is a simple skill to perfect and well worth the effort since it will eliminate a lot of turning and subsequent twisting and tangling of the yarns.

8 To knit in reverse (i.e., backwards), enter the stitch with the left needle tip from left to right, behind the right hand needle (8a). Wrap the yarn from back to front, coming up and over the left needle (8b). The yarn will slant up and to the left in the standard stitch mount position. Draw the yarn through to form the new loop on the left needle (8c). (Or, if combining Eastern and Western methods, the yarn, coming from under the needle, can be wrapped from front to back to form the stitches at the same gauge.) The motion for the left-hand carry in reverse is very similar to that of the right-hand carry in the

standard direction, requiring an overt wrapping move. The right-hand carry in reverse requires the flip of the finger to wrap the yarn, a motion similar to the left-hand carry in the standard direction.

The skills of *motif knitting*, especially in combination with reverse knitting, can be applied whenever contrast colors do not encircle the entire piece. Some of the Eastern socks have soles with patterning in a different color from that on the instep; other socks are color-stranded in two colors, but several other colors are worked only on the front of the foot/leg. For some of these patterns, the motif skills are important. For others the extra colors do not move across the entire front and working the front colors in zigzag intarsia is more applicable.

9 When working *zigzag intarsia* for pattern sections which do not encircle the foot/leg, the contrast section can be knit in standard color-stranding techniques, dropping the contrast yarn to the left of the section. Upon reaching that section on the next round, the contrast yarn is brought across the wrong side from left to right to bring it into position for color-stranding. When knitting with this zigzagging yarn, the best results are achieved by weaving the background color yarn behind every stitch. For larger blocks of color, I interlock the yarns before and after each section, as previously described with the *motif knitting*. Long zigzag

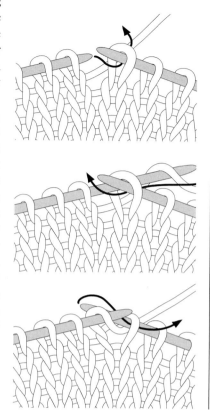

8 *Knitting in reverse*
a. To knit in reverse, enter back loop with left needle tip.

b. Wrap yarn from back to front over left needle tip.

c. While lifting right needle tip, draw wrap through and onto left needle to form new stitch.

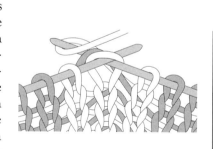

9 *Securing a zigzag float*
Enter stitch, then slip needle tip under float. Wrap yarn on needle, slip needle tip back under float and through stitch to complete new stitch. If float color shows through on front, work under float on next stitch also.

85

10

Twined knit stitches as a decorative element
This technique is typically used to outline a textured pattern. Two ends are twisted on back, then one brought forward while next stitch is worked with other yarn. Forward yarn then goes back to twist and second yarn is brought forward while next stitch is worked. The needle tip must pass between yarns before entering loop.

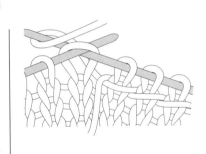

11

Twined purl stitches used as decorative braid
Since stitches are all purls, both yarns stay on the front, bring yarn over the strand worked on one round, under the strand worked on the next, with alternate stitches worked from the two yarns.

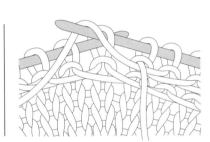

floats of the previous round can be secured when knitting across by first entering the stitch, then passing the needle tip under the float before wrapping the yarn. The wrap is then drawn under the float and through the existing loop to form the new loop.

Two-end knitting

Some textured socks and stockings are worked from two ends of the same ball. Unlike Scandinavian work, the two ends are not twisted when working in stockinette. Instead, the stitches are stranded, with alternate stitches coming from alternate ends of the same ball. Slightly more elastic than its twisted counterpart, the thickness is effectively doubled. This method is limited to the foot, heel, and ankle section with the leg in plain stockinette or textured patterns.

10 Some twined knitting is used for decorative purposes, on both knit and purl stitches. For *twined knit stitches*, often used as a subtle decorative element on the instep, the float is brought forward to ride on the surface over the knit stitch, most often as an outlining element. I find this work is most easily accomplished with both yarns in the right hand, one on each side of the forefinger. The two yarns are twisted clockwise on the back, the floating yarn then brought forward to the surface. The needle tip must be between the two yarns when the next loop is entered to knit. When the stitch is completed, the floating yarn

goes back to twist with the knitting yarn on back. The yarn that formed the last stitch then comes forward to form the float while the other yarn makes the next knit stitch.

11 *Twined purl stitches* are most often used as a small decorative braid to finish the top of the leg. These are often worked in two alternating colors when used in conjunction with a color-stranded design. Working the purl stitches in this manner is simple because the twist and float both occur on the front, eliminating the need to divide the yarns to front and back after twisting as with the knit. Usually, one round is worked by bringing the yarn under the strand worked, the next by bringing the yarn over the strand worked, all stitches purled. The float angles up and to the left when the yarn is brought over, up and to right when brought under the strand worked. By alternating rows, a decorative braid is achieved.

If working in contrasting colors, remember that the color of the previous knit row determines the colors of the purl head. Therefore, the colors must be set up on the knit row prior to working the twined purl stitches in contrast color. In some regions, knitters prefer to reverse their direction for the braid, turning to the backside and working it as knit stitches rather than purling.

Traveling stitches

Traveling stitches are usually connected with the Alpine knitting of Bavaria and Tyrol, but they are also practiced by some of the ethnic groups in these Eastern environs. In the Alpine style, the patterns are developed with twisted knit stitches traveling over a purl ground; in the East, standard knit stitches travel over a knit ground. Instead of the four moves (knit over knit, left and right, plus knit over purl, left and right), this style requires only two moves (knit over knit, left and right). In either case, the stitches can be worked out of order or the order can be reversed prior to working.

12 When working a *knit over knit to the right (1/1 RC)*, to work the *stitches out of order*, enter the second stitch on the left needle as to knit. Keeping the needle tip in front of the first stitch on the left needle, wrap and draw up the new loop. Do not remove the stitch just completed. Instead, enter the first stitch on the left needle and knit. Draw both stitches off together.

To work *the knit over knit to the left (1/1 LC) out of order*, the right needle tip must go behind the first stitch on the left needle, then come forward from back to front between the first and second stitches. The needle tip must then turn and enter the second stitch as to knit. When the stitch is knitted, the new loop must be carried out to the back, between the first and second stitches on the left needle. Again, the stitch is not removed. Instead, the right needle tip is brought around to the front to knit the first stitch on the left needle. Then, both stitches are removed together.

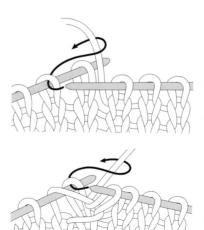

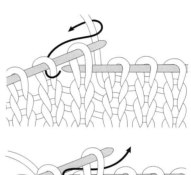

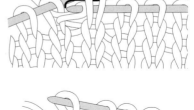

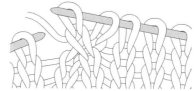

12

Traveling stitches worked out of order

Knit over knit, right
a. Enter second stitch on left needle in front as to knit. Knit this stitch but do not remove from left needle.

b. Enter first stitch in standard manner and knit. Draw two stitches off together.

Knit over knit, left
a. Bring needle behind first stitch, come forward between two stitches …

b. Enter second stitch in standard manner and knit. Do not remove stitch from needle. Take new stitch loop back between first and second stitches.

c. Knit first stitch. Draw two stitches off together.

87

13

Traveling stitches worked by changing the order of stitches

Knit over knit, right

a. Take right needle tip in front of first stitch, enter second stitch as to purl. Remove both stitches from left needle, freeing the first stitch.

b. Bring left needle tip across back to enter freed stitch from left to right.

c. Bring second stitch, now on right needle, across front of first stitch and place on left needle tip. Knit two stitches in new order.

Knit over knit, left

a. Take right needle tip behind first stitch to enter second stitch as to purl. Remove left needle from both stitches, freeing the first stitch.

b. Bring left needle tip across front to enter freed stitch from left to right.

c. Place second stitch, now on right needle, back onto left needle. Knit two stitches in new order.

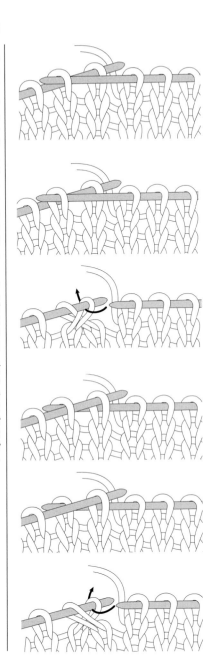

14

Bosnian slip stitch crochet

This is slip stitch crochet worked through back of chain head only. It builds horizontal rows on the socks.

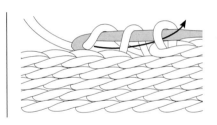

13

To change the order of the stitches for a knit over knit to the right (1/1 RC), take the right needle tip over the front of the first stitch on the left needle and enter the second stitch as to purl. Remove both stitches from the left needle, thus freeing the first stitch. Enter the freed stitch from left to right with the left needle tip. Bring the unworked second stitch now on the right needle tip across the front and place it on the tip of the left needle. The order of the two stitches has been reversed; they are ready to knit.

To work the knit over knit to the left (1/1 LC), take the right needle tip behind the first stitch on the left needle and enter the second stitch as to purl. Remove the left needle from both the first and second stitches, thus freeing the first stitch. Bringing the left needle tip around to the front, enter the freed stitch from left to right. Put the unworked stitch on the right needle tip back onto the left needle. The order of the stitches has now been reversed and they are ready to knit.

Some right-handed people prefer to slip both stitches to the right needle first, then change the order. The right-hand needle is then used to pick up the freed stitches.

Bosnian crochet

Sometimes referred to as Turkish crochet, *Bosnian crochet* is crochet worked through the middle of the crochet head, around the back loop only. When working within a knit structure, a row of Bosnian crochet is the same as the standard bind off in knitting.

14

Then, working through the middle of the crochet head (around back loop), round upon round of slip stitch crochet can be worked. When each round is worked in a new color, this will create horizontal lines of color around the stocking. When changing colors, remember that the loop on the needle (hook) will be the visible portion of the next stitch. Therefore, the color change must be set up in the previous loop.

For special decorative effects, usually centered on the instep or the leg front, a portion of the crochet round may have the entire crochet head exposed. This can be done by working the new stitches into the bar behind and below the chain head. Working in this manner will result in a section of full chain stitches between the horizontal lines of the standard Bosnian crochet.

15

Single crochet can also be worked Bosnian style. The single crochet is worked in the standard manner except that the hook again enters into the middle of the loop, thus creating the horizontal line. When changing colors in the typical Western manner, the new color is picked up in the last loop of the stitch, setting up the color for the next stitch. In most Bosnian crochet, the single crochet is usually completed before the color change. This carries the color into the next stitch, creating a broken color pattern.

The use of sections of Bosnian crochet within the knitted structure adds much visual interest. (And, when hooked knitting needles were common in the region, it was a relatively simple decorative technique.) The knitter can move from knitting to crochet between rounds and even within the round. Often, the instep may be worked in crochet, the sole in a separate pattern in knitting.

When crochet is used for the instep, the work can be continuous, working the instep in crochet and continuing the sole in knit. Or, the knit sole can be worked flat first, with the Bosnian crochet then joined at each end. If worked flat, the Bosnian crochet must be broken off at the end; it cannot be turned for a return row since the chain head would be on the wrong side of the fabric. However worked, with its inelastic nature, increasing at the ends of some of the crochet rows is necessary. When the leg of the sock is crocheted, it must be larger, and is often almost bootlike in appearance.

Bosnian crochet is often used as a decorative band to finish the leg of a sock. Again, its inelastic nature must be considered. The key to remember: the more closely packed the slip stitch crochet, the less elastic the fabric. This problem can be reduced by interspersing single crochet or knit rounds between the slip stitch rounds.

16 Not all horizontal lines of contrasting color are Bosnian crochet. In some cases, a tapestry needle is used to work an *outline stitch* around each knit stitch as a decorative element. The appearance is much the same as Bosnian crochet. When this method is used, a portion of the knit row is exposed between each horizontal color row. The contrast color yarn loops around each knit stitch.

Cross-stitch is also used to develop design on some of the stockings. For example, in Bulgaria cross-stitch occasionally replaces motif knitting when creating a pictorial motif on stockings.

A vertical row of *chain stitch* is occasionally used to incorporate a contrast color in the stocking. This appears very similar to a vertical row of knit stitches in a contrast color but eliminates the need to carry an additional color during construction. The contrast color yarn is placed inside the finished sock. A loop is drawn through to the surface with a hook, henceforth chained up and around the bar between the knit stitches.

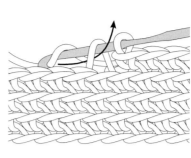

15
Bosnian single crochet
This is standard single crochet worked through back loop of chain head only. Enter back loop of chain head, draw up a loop.

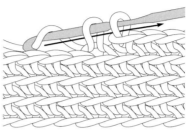

Then draw a new loop through both loops on hook.

16
Added embellishments

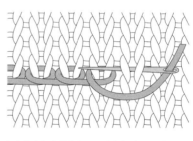

Outline stitch: using a threaded needle to create a horizontal line on the knit surface.

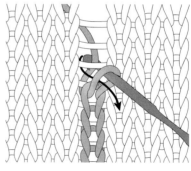

Vertical line of chain crochet worked over bar between stitches allows a vertical color contrast without carrying the contrast color while knitting.

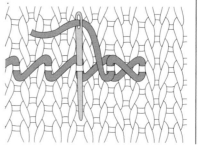

Cross-stitch embroidery

89

These small sampler socks were designed as learning pieces.
Each represents a full-sized traditional sock found in Chapter 2. Trying new
techniques is not as intimidating on this scale. And you can knit just one — no need for a pair.
LEFT TO RIGHT, Bulgarian floral sampler, Lur sampler, tufted toe sampler, and Caspian Sea sampler (pp. 92-95).

Chapter 5

Samplers

Our seven sampler socks cover much of the design and construction technique necessary to create socks in the Eastern tradition. Whether you go on to reproduce traditional pieces or design your own versions, these small socks are useful learning pieces. By trying them, you will not only perfect the techniques, but you will find the approaches you prefer.

These socks are knit from a range of handspun and millspun yarns in weights from fingering to sports weight, using size 2-3mm (American size 0-3) needles, as appropriate. For once gauge is not crucial.

The directions are general, not stitch-by-stitch, since that is the ethnic approach. Once again, italics denote techniques fully detailed in other chapters and listed in the index. Review these discussions as necessary, then apply what you've learned to these scaled-down but authentically detailed samplers.

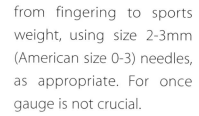

91

Samplers

W orsted-spun sports weight yarn, 3mm needles, 7½ stitches equal 1". The design techniques in this Bulgarian floral motif sock will serve you well; they can be used in many instances. The sock begins at the toe with a *figure-8 cast on* over 6 stitches, the toe is increased on every other round with the *make one, yarn over* to a total of 44 stitches.

When the toe is approximately 2" long, the floral motif is centered on the instep. While learning the two-step technique for *motif knitting*, I suggest that all the motif stitches be placed on one needle. With practice, you will find that it is easy to shift the motif from left to right on the needle, letting the color-stranded row end at the left of the pattern before changing needles and the two-step row end at the right. Thus, without repositioning the needles, there is basically a motif needle.

When the motif is complete, work 4 rounds, then knit *waste yarn* across the heel. Continue up the leg, positioning a motif on each side of the leg 1" above the waste yarn. Knit an additional inch and bind off.

Pick up the stitches for the *inserted heel* and remove the waste yarn. Pick up an extra stitch or two to close the gap at each side of heel and decrease them on the next round. Begin heel motif at center back. After 4 rounds, begin decreasing on every round to point of heel. When only a few stitches remain, break off and draw tail through remaining loops to close.

Main motif

Center st

1

The Bulgarian floral motif sampler uses basic Eastern toe to top construction. The main challenge is the two-step technique used for the floral motifs.

Heel motif

- ⬛ Blue
- ⬛ Green
- ⬜ Pink

Chapter 5

Worsted-spun sports weight yarn, 3mm needles, 7½ stitches equal 1". This Lur sock begins at the toe with a *straight wrap cast on* of 6 stitches. The cast on is arranged vertically, and a *rectangular flap* worked for *toe depth*. Since these toe depth/seam panel stitches are worked in pattern, the rectangle begins with one knit row, then a pattern round (p2, k2, p2) alternates with a knit round. After working 4 rounds thus to develop the rectangle, 3 top and 3 sole stitches are picked up on opposite sides of the rectangle (see Illustrations 4 on p. 65 and 16 on p. 71; arrange stitches as in 17b). Begin increasing 4 stitches every round, 1 stitch each side of each 6-stitch panel until there are 44 stitches. The textured side panels are the only design feature on the foot.

After 4" of knitting, work a *waste yarn* across the 22 sole stitches. Continue side panel in leg for an inch above the heel, then work the horizontal band and 3" of twisted rib. Finish top with one round of purl, one of knit, then bind off. Break yarn and draw through last loop — tail is not worked in.

Pick up heel stitches from waste yarn and work a *thumb-joint heel*. (The side panel pattern will be off by one-half stitch where the direction of knitting is reversed on the heel back.) Decrease 4 stitches each round (1 stitch on each side of each panel) until all stockinette stitches have been decreased. Graft panel stitches.

2

The Lur sock focuses on simple textured patterns, shaping between side panels, and a thumb-joint heel.

6-st side panel

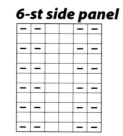

- ☐ = Purl
- ☐ = Knit
- ● = Twisted knit

Leg

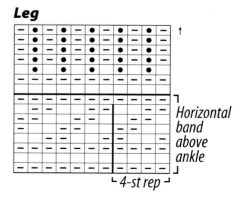

Horizontal band above ankle

4-st rep

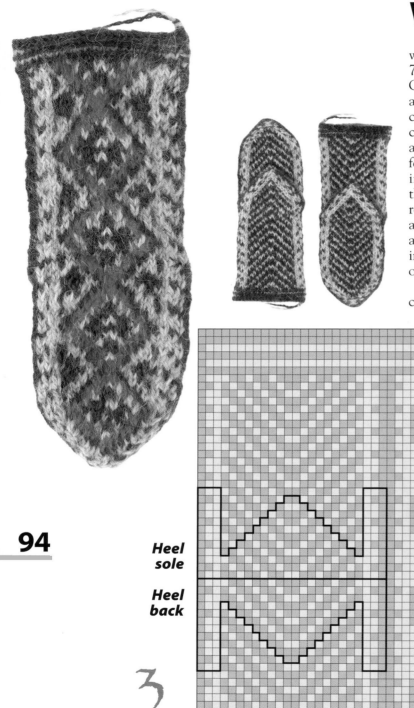

Woolen-spun sports weight yarn, 3mm needles, 7 stitches equal 1". This Caspian Sea sock begins with a *straight wrap cast on* in two colors (gray, purple, gray). The cast on is arranged vertically and a *rectangular flap* is worked for *toe depth*. The work begins immediately in pattern in the round. Once the initial rectangle is built, 2 stitches are picked up for the the top and sole of the toe and increasing begins on each side of the side panels.

When the third and fourth colors are introduced on the front of the sock, the two main colors continue in the round while the contrasting geometric patterning can be worked in *zig-zag intarsia* or *motif knitting*. If choosing the former, remember that long zigzag floats will cause tensioning problems. Therefore, the red diamonds should be worked from two yarns and each section of blue from a separate yarn.

When reaching the heel depth shown on chart, the sole stitches are placed on hold and the back leg stitches cast on with backward loops in the color pattern of the row being worked (see illustration 22, p. 74). This cast on is necessary in order to match color without the half-stitch jog when the direction of the knitting is reversed to knit the heel.

The leg of the sock is continued according to the chart, ending with single rounds of *Bosnian slip stitch crochet* on every other round and bound off in knit. Again, the tails are knotted and left exposed.

The *inserted heel* is then picked up in color pattern, working through the center of the backward loop cast on stitches. Decrease as indicated on the chart until only the side panels remain. Break off and lace yarn through the loops to draw up.

94

3

Interest builds in this Caspian Sea sock: the side panel is in two colors; the color pattern combines color-stranding with intarsia, the heel treatment allows for vertical patterning.

Heel sole

Heel back

—A
—A
—A

■ Blue ■ Purple
□ Gray ■ Red
A. Bosnian slip stitch crochet

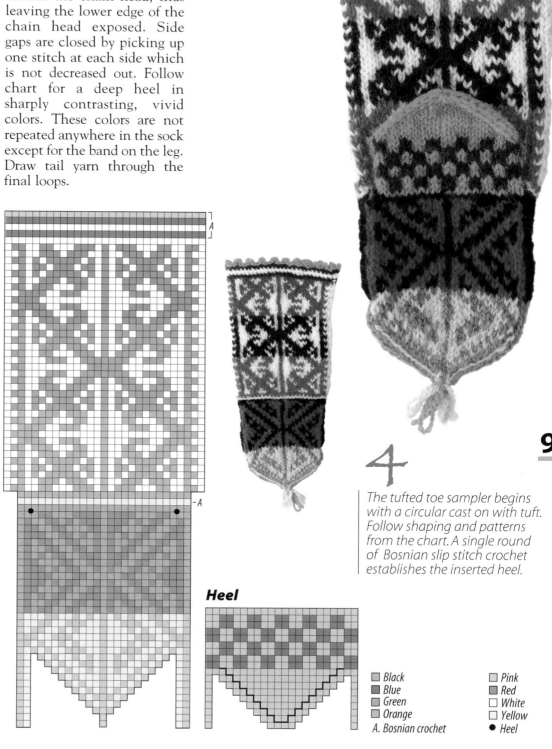

Woolen-spun Shetland weight yarn, 2.5mm needle, 8 stitches equal 1". This *tufted toe* stocking requires some dexterity in handling. (Remember, 10-stitch *circular cast on* can be worked without the tuft in the same way many circular shawls are begun.) On this stocking, the tuft is wrapped in pink and yellow, the stitch color sequence is pink, yellow, pink, yellow, pink on both the top and the sole (see Illustration 19, p. 72).

The knitting is simple *color-stranding* with increases on every round at each side of the 4 side panel stitches. Work to the heel position shown on the chart. The final round is knit in black then the sole stitches removed to a holder. Traditionally, less than half of the stitches are used for the heel of this sock (21 sts in this case). On the following round, the top instep stitches are bound off in yellow (*Bosnian crochet*) and the back stitches replaced: *crochet cast on at heel*.

The leg can be continued upward at this point or the heel outward. If continuing the leg, the stitches are picked up through the middle of the crochet (bind off) head in orange. On the next round, the leg is increased in pattern by two stitches on each needle. (The leg can be larger or smaller than the foot for this style of sock.) Follow the chart, ending in a band of *Bosnian crochet* as follows: one round of slip stitch crochet in blue, one round of single crochet in white, one round of slip stitch crochet in blue, the final round of crochet in pink

with a 3-chain crochet picot on every third stitch.

The *inserted heel* is then picked up through the bar behind the chain head, thus leaving the lower edge of the chain head exposed. Side gaps are closed by picking up one stitch at each side which is not decreased out. Follow chart for a deep heel in sharply contrasting, vivid colors. These colors are not repeated anywhere in the sock except for the band on the leg. Draw tail yarn through the final loops.

Heel

95

4

The tufted toe sampler begins with a circular cast on with tuft. Follow shaping and patterns from the chart. A single round of Bosnian slip stitch crochet establishes the inserted heel.

▨ Black	▨ Pink
▨ Blue	▨ Red
▨ Green	☐ White
▨ Orange	☐ Yellow
A. Bosnian crochet	● Heel

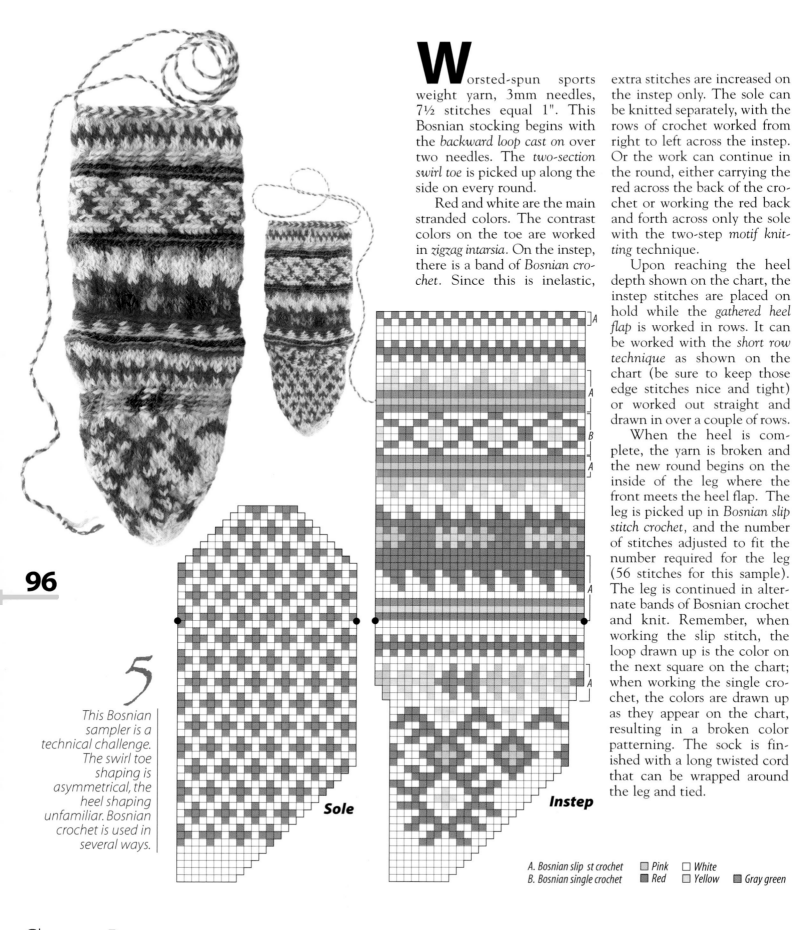

Worsted-spun sports weight yarn, 3mm needles, 7½ stitches equal 1". This Bosnian stocking begins with the *backward loop cast on* over two needles. The *two-section swirl toe* is picked up along the side on every round.

Red and white are the main stranded colors. The contrast colors on the toe are worked in *zigzag intarsia*. On the instep, there is a band of *Bosnian crochet*. Since this is inelastic, extra stitches are increased on the instep only. The sole can be knitted separately, with the rows of crochet worked from right to left across the instep. Or the work can continue in the round, either carrying the red across the back of the crochet or working the red back and forth across only the sole with the *two-step motif knitting* technique.

Upon reaching the heel depth shown on the chart, the instep stitches are placed on hold while the *gathered heel flap* is worked in rows. It can be worked with the *short row technique* as shown on the chart (be sure to keep those edge stitches nice and tight) or worked out straight and drawn in over a couple of rows.

When the heel is complete, the yarn is broken and the new round begins on the inside of the leg where the front meets the heel flap. The leg is picked up in *Bosnian slip stitch crochet*, and the number of stitches adjusted to fit the number required for the leg (56 stitches for this sample). The leg is continued in alternate bands of Bosnian crochet and knit. Remember, when working the slip stitch, the loop drawn up is the color on the next square on the chart; when working the single crochet, the colors are drawn up as they appear on the chart, resulting in a broken color patterning. The sock is finished with a long twisted cord that can be wrapped around the leg and tied.

96

5

This Bosnian sampler is a technical challenge. The swirl toe shaping is asymmetrical, the heel shaping unfamiliar. Bosnian crochet is used in several ways.

Sole

Instep

A. Bosnian slip st crochet
B. Bosnian single crochet

	Pink		White
	Red		Yellow
			Gray green

Worsted-type sports weight yarn, 3mm needles, 7½ stitches equal 1". The foot of this Bakhtiari stocking is worked in *two-end knitting*.

Begin at the toe with a *straight wrap cast on* over 6 stitches. The cast on is arranged vertically and a *rectangular flap* is worked for *toe depth*. Working in the round, knit one stitch from one ball and the next stitch with the second ball. After working 2-3 rounds, 2 top and 2 sole stitches are picked up on opposite sides of the rectangle. Arrange stitches as shown in Illustration 17b, p. 71. Begin increasing 4 stitches every round, 1 stitch each side of the initial 6-stitch side panels.

When there are 48 stitches, begin the 'ridge' on top of the instep: twist the two working yarns and knit 4 stitches from one yarn, then draw the second yarn tightly across the back and resume two-end knitting. When the toe is 2" long, work the charted instep pattern of *twined knit stitches*.

When the sock measures 4", place the sole stitches on hold and cast on with backward loops above with the two yarns to continue the leg (see Illustration 22, p. 74). Two-end knitting is continued for 1" up the leg. The *traveling stitch* band is then worked in one yarn only, followed by 4½" of twisted rib and one purl round (see p. 116 for help reading the chart). Bind off in knit. The tail is drawn through to secure the final loop and allowed to hang free.

Heel stitches are picked up and worked out, maintaining the ridge at center back. After two rounds, decrease 1 stitch on each side of each side panel every round. When only panel stitches remain, graft panel stitches.

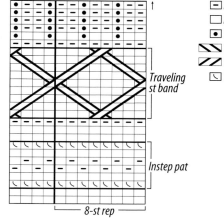

Key:
- ⊟ Purl
- ☐ Knit
- ⊡ Twisted knit
- ⧄ 1/1 LC
- ⧅ 1/1 RC
- ⊿ Twined st

Traveling st band

Instep pat

8-st rep

The foot of this Bakhtiari stocking is worked in two-end knitting for extra thickness. A variation in the technique forms a decorative ridge. Twined and traveling stitches are used in the ankle band.

Dense worsted-spun fingering weight yarn, 2.5mm needles, 7½ stitches equal 1". Traditionally, the *tubular strip toe for a square toe* makes a long, somewhat narrow, tapered foot. When knitting a real sock, the increases can be closely spaced at the toe for a more comfortable fit.

The initial cast on is worked with a *backward loop* since the colors must be matched at the end when circular knitting begins (see Illustration 20, p. 73). Cast on 1 red stitch, 2 black, 1 red and knit the strip for ten rows as shown on the chart. These rows can all be knitted: at the end of a row, don't turn work, carry the yarn loosely across the back, and knit in the same direction. (Or the strip can be worked flat, knitting and purling the rows).

The work then begins in the round by rotating the strip to pick up 9 stitches along the edge of the rectangle, rotate to pick up and knit into the initial backward loop stitches, then rotate to pick up 9 stitches along the opposite side of the rectangle.

Work color pattern from the chart, increasing as shown. The two side vertical patterns are worked in *zigzag intarsia*, woven over one of the two main colors. This is easily accomplished if the main color yarn is held in the left hand and the vertical panel yarns in the right hand. Thus, the red and green yarns at each side are not carried around. The patterning on the front foot/ leg and back leg can be worked

in either *zigzag intarsia* or *motif intarsia*. If working in zigzag intarsia, the green diagonals should be worked with two separate yarns since the long floats could distort the design.

At the heel, the sole stitches are knit on a *waste yarn* and the leg continued upward. The leg is worked according to the chart, ending with two rounds of *twined purl* in red and green, matching color to color. It is then bound off in red and green. A short twisted cord is made of the tail yarns, ending in a tassel in red and green.

The *inserted heel* is picked up and worked in black for two rounds. (Since the pattern changes at the heel, it was not necessary to use a backward loop cast on.) The heel is decreased on every round to a point as shown on chart. The last loops are drawn together, the tail yarn pulled through in a loop, tied off with the tail, and allowed to hang free.

7

This little sock is an intarsia sampler. Maintain side panels in color pattern while you work geometric motifs in zigzag intarsia.

BO
Twined purl

Divide for Heel •

• (center divide mark)

CO

↑ Begin Rnd after strip →

Heel

• Heel

☐- Purl
■ Black

■ Red
■ Green

☐ White
☐ Yellow

Whether knit from the top down or the toe up, whether gusseted
or not, socks — both East and West — are made to be worn on variously-sized
but similarly-shaped feet. Traditional Eastern socks play footsie with a modern hybrid: LOWER RIGHT
HAND CORNER its toe is Turkish, the heel extension Bulgarian, the heel shaping Iranian, and the stripes Guatemalan.

East meets West

Reproduction of old ethnic folkwear is not always practical. Often, it must be adapted to fit modern styles of life and dress. This is certainly true of Eastern ethnic socks and stockings.

For wearers of Birkenstocks or clogs, both similar to the traditional type of shoes of much of the region, these socks are superb in their traditional form. But, for a typical Western shoe, only some of the less elaborate socks patterned with horizontal bands or with intarsia-type motifs, traditionally worn with a moccasin-type slipper, may be appropriate. Of course, any can be worn as a house sock. In fact, many were traditionally worn indoors without shoes (which helps to explain why so much effort would go into patterning the sole).

All the socks shown in this chapter use the hybrid pattern that I have developed. It is really an Eastern sock adapted for modern, Western wear. The inspiration for the toe is Turkish, the heel extension is Bulgarian, and the heel shaping Iranian. Our examples are socks with simple or no patterning, but the hybrid can also be used as a sizing and shaping guide for more elaborately patterned socks similar to those in Chapter 2.

101

How to's

Why a gusset? 1   **Fitting an Eastern sock** 2   **East/West hybrids** 3, 4, 5

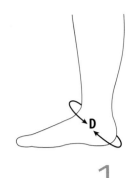

1

Why a gusset?
Diagonal circumference
around heel (D) is much greater
than the straight circumference
at either the ball of the foot
or the ankle.

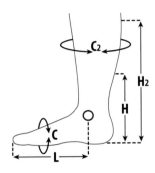

102

2

Fitting an Eastern sock
Measure C (circumference at
ball of foot) and L (length of
foot from the tip of the toe to
the point of the ankle). For a
stocking, also measure H
(height from floor to point
where girth of leg begins to
increase, C2 (circumference of
calf), and H2 (height from
floor to top of stocking).

1 Why are Eastern ethnic socks not suitable for most everyday wear? Primarily, because of fit. Western socks have a gusset; Eastern socks do not. This is a significant difference. The diagonal circumference (D) around the heel to the top of the foot is much greater than the straight circumference at either the ball of the foot or the ankle. Without the extra ease provided by the extra stitches in the gusset, the elasticity of the ankle portion of the sock must accommodate the wearer's heel. This is primarily a problem with some *inserted heels* and can be alleviated by working the *thumb-joint heel* extension before decreasing on the heel. Or, a *heel flap* can be extended sufficiently to eliminate the problem since the length of the flap determines the circumference of the leg.

Design further complicates fit. Any time a color-stranded pattern is incorporated in a sock, whether Western or Eastern in concept, ease must be increased. A typical Western sock will require an increase of no more than 10%; an Eastern style might need 15% or more if worked in the traditional manner. When many colors are used in the design, often with long carries, elasticity is tremendously reduced. The longer the carries, the less the elasticity of the knit structure. A typical Western design has relatively short floats; an Eastern design often has extensive floats. As a result these socks, of necessity, fit more loosely: the less elastic the structure, the wider

the ankle and leg must be. A good example is the Bosnian sock: richly embellished with *Bosnian crochet* and almost boot-like in appearance to have sufficient width to accommodate the passage of the foot. Even with the looser fit, it can require a considerable 'tug' to pull on these socks. Once the foot has settled into the heel of the sock, it is quite comfortable, but getting there can take some effort.

The lack of elasticity is heightened by the tight gauge at which the traditional Eastern socks and stockings are worked. This can be relieved by knitting at a somewhat looser gauge, more in keeping with modern knitting. But this reduces the number of stitches available for design development unless a finer yarn is used. A loose gauge also compromises a sock's durability.

2 Fitting the Eastern sock is incredibly easy. A sock requires only two measurements for a custom fit. The first is the circumference around the ball of the foot (C). If working in stockinette in one color, the actual measurement will give a generous fit; reduce by 5-10% for a snug fit. Determine the length of the foot (L) before dividing for the heel. Again, reduce 5-10% if a snug fit is desired. To conform to the foot, the heel should be extended before decreasing. The *thumb-joint heel* rule applies, but I use 10-15% of the length from toe to ankle to eliminate any guesswork.

If a stocking is desired, two additional measurements are helpful. The distance before increasing is approximately 1" more than length (L). To custom fit, measure the height from the floor to the point where the girth of the leg begins to increase (H); this is where increasing becomes necessary. How much to increase is determined by the circumference of the calf (C2). The final measurement would be the total height from floor to top of stocking (H2).

For design development, I find starting at the toe decidedly advantageous. A Western sock must be carefully planned to determine where the pattern ends when reaching the toe. An Eastern sock can be more easily adapted since the total length is flexible; the sock can be ended when it is visually appropriate. Or, if working in authentic Eastern mode, the design simply ends whenever the proper length is reached!

The speed with which socks can be knit is often noted as one of the reasons the American knitter is interested in making them. None of the Eastern ethnic socks and stockings are speedy. They require a commitment of time and energy: first to develop the technical skills (spinning and/or knitting) to pursue traditional designs, then to carry through and produce the socks or stockings desired. But, remember, they are small projects and thus readily transported. A few minutes here, a few minutes there, and soon a pair is finished. A tremendous sense of accomplishment accompanies each finished piece. The intricate designs in dazzling color combinations are astounding.

Of course, there is always the possibility of applying some of the Eastern design concepts to a Western structure. Or adopt the simplicity of the Eastern structure with less design — say, a plain foot so a snug fit can be accommodated. But one thing is clear: understanding the Eastern concepts of both design and construction will broaden the scope of Western knitting even if never used in the traditional ways.

East/West hybrids

Eastern knitting designs and techniques have certainly altered my approach to the craft and expanded my horizons both technically and creatively. But change is inevitable, even with the socks we wear. What was appropriate then is not necessarily desirable here and now. With this in mind, I selected my favorite structural components from the many Eastern options and developed a composite sock that suits my needs relative to shape, fit, and ease of construction. In this hybrid the inspiration for the toe comes from Turkey, the heel extension from Bulgaria, the heel shaping from Iran — with minor adjustments in increasing and decreasing to achieve the desired fit.

With two measurements, the circumference and length of foot, the hybrid sock can be made to fit anyone. The following instructions encourage an ethnic, plan-your-own approach to knitting. A concise chart gives stitch numbers for socks knit in several weights of yarn in

a complete range of sizes. On the next two pages are examples of three simple hybrid socks.

3 *Cast on:* To begin this sock, I use a *straight wrap cast on* (unless multiple colors require casting on with backward loops). The number of stitches to cast on depends on the weight of the yarn. Cast on an even number of stitches for a strip that is about one-half inch wide for a child's sock, one-half to three-quarters inch wide for a woman's sock, three-quarters to one inch for a man's.

Begin the toe: This strip is knit back and forth (knit one row, purl the next) until the number of rows equals 150 to 200% of the number of stitches in the strip's width.

The strip will wrap around the toe, with the instep and sole stitches picked up along each side of the strip, one stitch at the end of every other row. If an even number of stitches is required, the number of rows must be divisible by 4. If a center stitch is required for the pattern, the number of rows must be divisible by 4 plus or minus 2 stitches. For example: a cast-on of 8 stitches would require 12 rows (150% of 8) for an even number of stitches for top and bottom (6 stitches) and 10 rows for an odd number (5 stitches). A cast-on of 6 stitches would require 8 rows for an even number, 10 rows for an odd number (150% of 6=9).

When the strip is worked to the desired length, begin knitting in the round. At this point, there will be a needle at

103

Size group	Size of sock	Initial rectangle			Toe shaping		Heel shaping				Yarn
		Stitches to cast on	Rows to work	Stitches to pick up	Inc every row to	Inc every other row to	Heel sts on hold	Dec every row to	Dec every other row to	Seam stitches to graft	
SMALL	6	6	12	6		56	28	42	20	4	Light sock 9.5 sts/inch — 4-6 ozs
SMALL	6½	6	12	6		60	30	44	20	4	
SMALL	7	6	12	6		64	32	48	20	4	
MEDIUM	7½	8	12	6	54	72	36	54	24	6	
MEDIUM	8	8	12	6	60	76	38	60	24	6	
MEDIUM	8½	8	12	6	64	80	40	64	24	6	
LARGE	9	10	16	8	64	84	42	64	28	8	
LARGE	9½	10	16	8	68	88	44	68	28	8	
LARGE	10	10	16	8	72	92	46	72	28	8	
SMALL	6	6	12	6		48	24	36	20	4	Medium sock 8 sts/inch — 6-8 ozs
SMALL	6½	6	12	6		52	26	40	20	4	
SMALL	7	6	12	6		56	28	44	20	4	
MEDIUM	7½	8	12	6	44	60	30	44	24	6	
MEDIUM	8	8	12	6	48	64	32	48	24	6	
MEDIUM	8½	8	12	6	52	68	34	52	24	6	
LARGE	9	8	16	8	56	72	36	56	28	6	
LARGE	9½	8	16	8	60	76	38	60	28	6	
LARGE	10	8	16	8	64	80	40	64	28	6	
SMALL	6	4	8	4		40	20	32	12	2	Heavy sock 6.5 sts/inch — 8-10 ozs
SMALL	6½	4	8	4		40	20	36	12	2	
SMALL	7	4	8	4		44	22	40	12	2	
MEDIUM	7½	6	8	4	36	48	24	36	16	4	
MEDIUM	8	6	8	4	40	52	26	40	16	4	
MEDIUM	8½	6	8	4	44	56	28	44	16	4	
LARGE	9	6	12	6	44	56	28	44	20	4	
LARGE	9½	6	12	6	48	60	30	48	20	4	
LARGE	10	6	12	6	52	64	32	52	20	4	
SMALL	6	2	4	2		30	15	22	6	2	*Boot sock 5 sts/inch — 10-12 ozs
SMALL	6½	2	4	2		32	16	24	6	2	
SMALL	7	2	4	2		36	18	24	6	2	
MEDIUM	7½	4	8	4	26	38	19	26	12	2	
MEDIUM	8	4	8	4	32	40	20	32	12	2	
MEDIUM	8½	4	8	4	34	42	21	34	12	2	
LARGE	9	4	8	4	36	44	22	36	12	2	
LARGE	9½	4	8	4	36	48	24	36	12	2	
LARGE	10	4	8	4	38	50	25	38	12	2	

Sizing: Large (men), Medium (youth/women), Small (children). Small socks are not anatomically shaped. Yarn quantities apply to a pair of adult socks in one color.

*Due to a limited number of stitches on the Boot sock, some sizes will require an odd number of stitches on front and back, and Small sizes will have same number of stitches at heel and toe.

3

East/West hybrid crew socks

The inspiration for this hybrid's toe comes from Turkey, the heel extension from Bulgaria, and the heel shaping from Iran. Its modified toe shaping produces a sock for the left and the right foot. Two measurements — the circumference of the foot and the length of the foot — are all that's needed for this custom fit. If you prefer not to do the math, follow the chart on the preceding page.

each end of the strip. Rotate work to side of rectangle and, with a third needle, pick up and knit in the middle of the stitch at the end of every other row. Rotate work to knit across the initial cast-on stitches. Rotate, repeat the pickup and knit along the final edge.

The work is now in a rectangle. Reposition the stitches to divide in the middle of the cast on stitches at each end and in the middle of the top and bottom stitches (unless pattern requires an odd number). This arranges the stitches as a *vertical cast on*; designate the middle of the end stitches as the beginning of round.

Shaping the toe: The toe can be increased at each side seam panel on every other round for a standard symmetrical shape. I prefer to shape the toe for a left and right sock. For this anatomical shape, increase on each side of the seam panel on every round until 75-80% of the total number of stitches required in the circumference is reached. Henceforth, increase on every other round on the outside edge only (the little toe side) until the total number of stitches in the circumference is reached. For a blunt toe, continue to increase on every round.

Foot: The foot is knit even on these stitches to the required length. (For a snug fit, reduce L by 5-10%.) At this point, divide the work for an *inserted heel*. The *waste yarn* method is appropriate unless the design requires the *backward loop cast on* for a vertical pattern match. If the yarn is very fine with many stitches to the inch, use the invisible cast-on for the back leg.

Leg: For a standard crew sock with ribbing, continue working in stockinette stitch as established until the ankle section reaches a length equal to 10-15% of the total length of the foot (L). For example: If the foot length is 7", knit in stockinette for ¾-1". Begin a knit 2, purl 2 rib. Work to desired length, usually 10-15% longer than the foot length.

Heel: To insert the heel, pick up stitches and work outward, making a thumb-joint extension prior to shaping. Rather than estimating, knit the extension to a length equal to 10-15% of the foot length (L).

The heel is shaped at each side of a side panel as was the toe. To visually balance the increase and decrease, the heel panel should be two stitches less than the panel at the toe. For an 8-stitch panel at the toe, use a 6-stitch panel at the heel; for 6 at toe, use 4 at heel. Begin to decrease on every other round at each side of the seam panels until 75-80% of the stitches remain. Then, decrease every round until the number of stitches on heel back and sole equals that of the stitches on instep and sole of toe on the initial round.

To close the heel, work back and forth across the side panel, slipping the first stitch of every row. Remove one heel back stitch at one side and a heel sole stitch at the other. Decrease as follows: SSK when knitting, purl 2 together when purling. When all heel stitches have been decreased in this manner, graft the side panels.

Reverse shaping for second sock.

These socks, knit by the East/West hybrid pattern, draw from diverse cultures and are decidedly ethnic in appearance. They are worked in stockinette, a stitch not as elastic as the 2/2 rib used for the leg of the hybrid crew sock. On the Guatemalan sock, I increased 1 stitch on each needle when the leg length equaled the foot length (folded at the heel). The colored stripes are 3 rounds each, the black 2 rounds. The top is finished with 8 rows of garter stitch and bound off.

A short twisted cord is drawn behind 2 stitches, tied in a square knot, and tassels tied at the ends.

The Southwestern sock design is based on the 'Ganado Red' Navajo rug, a regional style of northwestern Arizona. This simple design is perfect for those who wear open-backed shoes and allows practice with motif knitting. I increased for the leg on each needle, once an inch before the design band at the top and again on the row below the band. The top of the leg, with 3 widely-spaced rounds of purl, tends to roll slightly — as is typical of many Eastern socks. When on the leg, the roll disappears.

I ended with a twisted cord in the two colors, leaving a 4" length to knot and tassel. These cords begin and end at the inside of the leg where the tassel covers the beginning of round. The cords can be tied together and used to hang the socks.

4
Guatemalan socks

5
Southwest socks

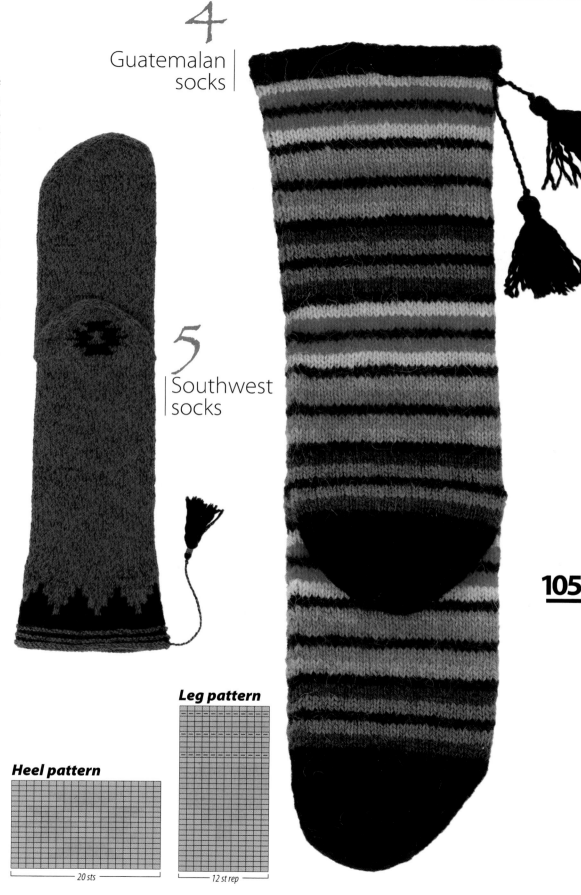

Heel pattern

— 20 sts —

Leg pattern

— 12 st rep —

105

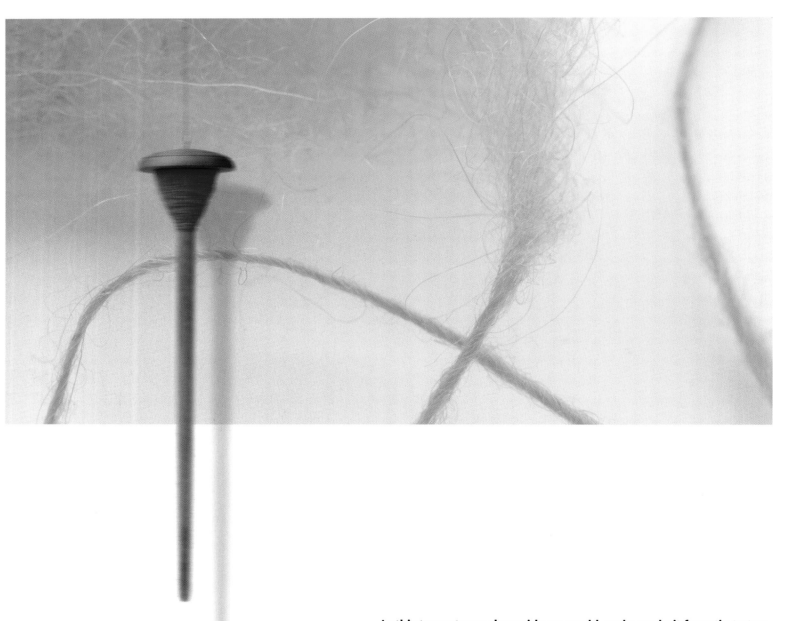

In this topsy-turvy, downside-up world, socks are knit from tip to top, and spindles stand on their heads. Surprisingly, both reversals make sense — the socks fit, the high whorl spindle turns fiber into strong yarn suitable for socks.

Yarns

Traditionally, all the Eastern yarns were spun on hand spindles. Throughout this entire region, spinning wheel technology was not widely embraced. Eastern Europe was a rural, agrarian society known for its resistance to change, proud of its ethnic and folk art heritage. Moving eastward, the region was still largely agrarian, with a large semi-nomadic to nomadic population typical of the more arid lands. The lifestyle and limited resources restricted the acquisition of household goods to small, portable items, more often than not, homemade. The hand spindle had served this population well through the centuries and continued to do so into the 20th century.

In some of the rural villages of the Balkans, spinning continues as a normal pursuit in daily life. Beautiful handspun socks and stockings are still obtainable. But with the changing political climate and the push to modernization, this cannot last. By the 1970's, the nomadic way of life was discouraged, and large numbers of village people flocked to the urban areas. They took their crafts with them, but these were soon altered in form. Today, one seldom sees handspun wool or even commercial wool yarns.

Some understanding of spinning and handspun yarn is important for both spinners and non-spinners. This information is valuable to those seeking suitable commercially-spun yarns. A brief sketch of the process of using the high whorl hand spindle can serve both as an introduction for those unfamiliar with hand spinning and give sufficient information for those who want to begin producing their own ethnic style sock yarn.

107

How to's

Selecting the wool

As with most peasant populations, the spinner-knitter of this region used the wool that was locally available. In fact many of the older pieces, particularly from Turkey, are made of a hairy wool, quite scratchy in hand. The limited literature available on the knitting yarns of the region refer to the wool from three types of sheep: curly-fleeced sheep, fat-tailed sheep, and crossbreeds thereof. Obviously, these are very broad categories. The curly-fleeced sheep produce a softer, silky medium wool of good staple length while the fat-tailed sheep produce either long, lustrous, strong wool or dual-coated wool (a soft, wooly undercoat in combination with a long outercoat).

Today's handspinners can pick and choose their wool and are no longer limited by local availability. The best fiber for sock yarn is both soft and silky for comfort against the skin and long and strong for durability. Rather than seeking to duplicate the traditional yarns with the breed of the region, suitable wools available from premium wool growers should be considered — both the medium wools for comfort and the long wools for durability. Other important characteristics are wools that have a soft sheen to good luster and accept dyes well. And, for me, selecting breeds which produce a good range of natural colors is important; many of my beautiful 'old' colors are achieved by top-dyeing natural colored wools. A further criterion to consider is fleece that is easy to process for handcrafting. Not all the possibilities will be considered, only those with which I have personal experience and have found to be desirable.

For those who put the comfort factor foremost, two ancient breeds, both of Scandinavian origin, must be evaluated: the Finnsheep (Finnish Landrace) of Finland and the Gotland (Palssau) of Sweden. Both are silky medium wools with a subtle sheen. Both have proven suitable for handcrafting in Scandinavia where the textile arts remained viable throughout the period of industrialization. The Finnsheep produces an open fleece that is easy to process even for the beginner. It is one of my favorites for a wide range of uses, including socks for sensitive skin. The Gotland, with incredibly silky fibers (especially yearling fleece) is somewhat harder to handle. It is probably the least irritating to the skin but is renowned for its propensity to felt. In the soles, felting must be expected. Neither offers the highest possible level of durability, but this can be mitigated in the preparation for spinning (i.e., by combing rather than carding).

Among the long, luster wools, both Lincoln and Romney have much to offer the handcrafter. Both wools are easy to handle and accept dyestuffs in brilliant hues. These wools are much stronger fiber with a long staple, so offer the greatest durability. Since they are coarse, often suitable for rugs, care must be taken to select only those fleeces with finer fibers for socks and stockings. Even so, this type of wool may prove to be uncomfortable for people with very sensitive skin. This is especially true in a worsted preparation. Although the yarn will have a smooth surface, the fiber ends are somewhat prickly because the dense, highly twisted fibers cannot 'give' as they can in a woolen preparation.

A suitable compromise to consider is a crossbred fleece, such as the Finn-Lincoln. The resulting fleece can offer the best of two breeds — the softness of the Finn with the durability of the Lincoln — yet retain luster. With a good range of natural colors, this is probably my favorite for sock yarns. But, in seeking a crossbred wool, bear in mind that the fleece of a crossbreeding program can be unpredictable. Each fleece must be considered on its own merits.

Lastly, the ancient *dual-coated wools* are a possibility. Here you have a fleece that has both the soft wool and the long wool in one package. The finer undercoat softens the yarn and provides a cushioning spring while the outer fibers provide the durability. Breeds that fall into this category are the Karakal (Uzbekistan), Spelsau (Norway), and Navajo-churro (a derivative of the original churro of the American Southwest). From these primitive breeds, one is guaranteed a more primitive quality in the yarn. Being from the Southwest, I am particularly fond of the Navajo-churro. Plus, the lack of grease makes it easy to process. But, these wools are not a suitable choice for socks to be worn next to sensitive skin.

Preparing the fleece

The processing of the fleece begins with *sorting*. As the term implies, the fleece is divided into sections with the same characteristics, for the fibers vary from one part of the body to another. When all fibers of similar characteristics are grouped together, the wool is *scoured*. The scouring process is not as harsh as it sounds, but rather a very gentle cleansing with a mild, neutral detergent.

After drying, the clean wool is ready for the final preparation step. The wool can be *carded* to spin a *woolen yarn*, or it can be *combed* to spin a *worsted yarn*. These are two very different techniques and result in two distinctively different yarns.

A *woolen* yarn is typically made from the shorter wools. None of the fibers is removed, therefore many fiber lengths are present in the final yarn. The fibers are carded to open and align them. Spun with low twist, the resulting yarn can be very light and lofty, since shorter wools have tight crimp that enhances airiness. These yarns are the warmest possible per unit weight, but they are not highly durable nor pill resistant. All the wools discussed can be carded for sock yarns, but they should not be spun in the classic woolen system. Even though carded, they should be spun worsted style to enhance durability.

The *carders* have a special 'cloth' attached to a wooden backing. The card cloth is embedded with many fine metal teeth, much like some pet brushes. The wool is brushed between two carders during preparation.

1 Before carding, the wool is *teased* to open the locks, then placed on the carder. Use a small amount of wool; overloading is inefficient and results in poorly carded wool. Holding the cards with handles pointed in opposite directions, the fibers are passed from one carder to the other by stroking the top carder over the bottom carder.

2 When most of the fibers have transferred to the top carder, the fibers are transferred back to the bottom carder and the process repeated.

3 The carding process is not harsh, but rather a gentle brushing. When most fibers have again transferred, the remaining fibers on the bottom carder are transferred to the top carder and the process repeated. Carding continues in this manner until the fibers are sufficiently prepared.

1

Loading the carder
First the wool is teased to open the locks. The teased wool is lightly brushed onto the surface of the card cloth, just to catch the fibers onto the metal teeth of the bottom carder.

2

Transferring to bottom carder
The fibers pass from the bottom to the top carder. To transfer them back to the bottom: invert the top carder, positioning it above the bottom carder so that the fiber fringe catches in the upper row of teeth. Press the edge of the top carder onto the bottom carder. Release pressure, raising the bottom carder to lift the fiber batt from top carder.

109

3

Transferring to top carder
As carding continues, most fibers pass to the top carder. To transfer the remaining fibers to the top carder, invert the top carder, positioning the fringe on the bottom carder onto the upper rows of the top carder. Press edge of bottom carder (now above top carder), release pressure, raising the top carder to lift the fiber batt.

4

Rolling a rolag
The fibers are first lifted off of the top carder, then the bottom (as if transferring). With fibers thus freed, the fibers can be rolled lengthwise up the face of the cloth. This tube is called a rolag.

5

Folding a batt
The fibers are released from the card cloth as before. The batt is folded across the face of the cloth, maintaining the alignment necessary to simulate a combed preparation for spinning.

6

Loading a comb
Clean, open locks are loaded, just catching the fibers on the wool comb. The tines of a hand-held comb can be loaded from 1/3 to 1/2 of their length.

110

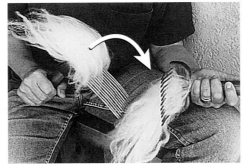

7

Vertical combing stroke
With stationary comb held on its side in the left hand, tines pointing away, the moving comb in right hand is passed downward in a circular motion, catching into the fringe of fibers. With each stroke, the tines move farther into the fiber mass. Continue until all fibers have been transferred to comb in right hand. Clean short fibers from comb in left hand.

4 When the carding is completed, for a true *woolen yarn*, the fibers are rolled into a rolag, rolling the fibers up lengthwise across the carder face, creating a lofty tube. A yarn spun from this package is not suitable for socks.

5 For a worsted-type yarn, the fibers are folded crosswise across the face of the carder, keeping the fibers in general alignment. This folded batt can then be attenuated into a roving. Yarn spun from this preparation will be dense, durable, and suitable for socks.

A true *worsted yarn* is spun from wool fibers that have been combed. Combing the wool removes all the shorter fibers, leaving only the long fibers in parallel alignment. Yarns spun from this preparation are more lustrous since light is reflected from the smooth surface. The long fibers have less crimp and therefore pack together when spun, thus forming a dense yarn. This yarn is extremely durable and pill resistant. A worsted yarn is considered the best sock yarn. But, being dense, it does not offer much cushioning to the foot. The *dual-coated wools* are not good candidates for combing, because the combing process will separate the two coats.

There are many types of wool combs, from those with several rows of tines (multi-pitch) which require a fixed combing station to those with only one or two rows of tines (single and double pitch) that

are hand held. The latter is the type more typical in the peasant home.

6 To comb, locks of wool are gently opened and loaded onto one comb. Many purists insist that the wool be loaded only at the cut end. This requires very careful scouring, not a process that lends itself to the peasant surroundings. Therefore, I mix the loading between cut ends and tips.

7 The wool is loaded on the stationary comb and combed to the moving comb, then back to the stationary comb. Holding the left comb (stationary comb) with tines pointing away and the right comb (moving comb) with tines down, begin combing the ends of the fibers. With each stroke, the comb moves farther into the fiber supply. The fibers will pass to the right comb. When all the long fibers have transferred to the right comb, any short fibers and debris are cleaned from the left comb.

8 Maintaining the same position with the combs, but using a horizontal movement, the fibers are passed back onto the left comb. The wool is passed from left to right, right to left, until the preparation is satisfactory.

9 The wool is then drawn off the comb into a long strand called a top. It is ready for spinning a *worsted yarn*. Until ready to spin, the top can be

gently wrapped around the fingers into a 'nest' for storage.

There is a third option for preparation: hand manipulation of the fibers using no tools. The fibers are opened, aligned, and spun directly from the lock in a worsted style. Although a method practiced by peasants, it is not a method that I recommend unless working with a very high quality, clean fleece.

Spinning the yarn

As stated earlier, the hand spindle was the tool of choice for this region. As in other parts of the world, many types of hand spindles were used. And the hand spindles were manipulated in various ways, depending upon local preferences, fiber selected, and yarn desired. I will consider only one type, the one which I consider most suitable for production of sock yarns.

Today, most handspinners learn to spin on a hand spindle — and move on to a spinning wheel as soon as skills and finances allow. This is regrettable because the hand spindle, especially a high whorl hand spindle, has so much to offer. It is inexpensive, portable, easy to use, and highly versatile.

Hand spindles can be used in two ways, either suspended or supported. A *suspended spindle* is just that, hanging by the yarn in progress. This type of hand spindle is often referred to as a 'drop spindle' — a somewhat negative connotation that tends to prove itself. A *supported spindle* rests on something: on the ground, in a bowl, or on the thigh. A good example of this kind of spindle, familiar to many, is the Navajo spindle.

A spindle has two parts: the *shaft* and *whorl*. The whorl enhances the rate of rotation. The low whorl is the most readily recognized as it is the most common type used historically in the English-speaking parts of the world. The whorl is located at the base of the shaft, with the top of the shaft notched for securing the yarn with a half hitch. The spinner twirls the spindle by hand, then draws out the fibers while allowing twist to enter. At the end of each spinning, the half hitch is removed, the yarn wound onto the spindle, the half hitch replaced and the spinning resumed. For many, this is a slow, tedious process because of the need for the half hitch. For others, the twirling process with the hand becomes most uncomfortable, especially for arthritic joints.

The high whorl spindle is less well known, but historically was used in many regions of the world, from Iceland to Scandinavia in the north, to Greece and the Balkans in the south, then eastward into Turkey and the Middle East. In this case, the whorl is located at the top of the shaft where there is a hook to secure the yarn for spinning. The hook eliminates the half hitch process. And, instead of twirling by hand, the spindle is rolled on the thigh to set it into motion. Depending on the type of yarn desired, it can be held suspended (as for sock yarns) or it can remain supported on the thigh (for softly

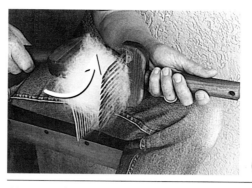

8

Horizontal combing stroke
With a horizontal circular stroke, the comb in right hand strokes the fibers onto the comb in left hand, starting at the fringe and moving up into the fiber mass until all fibers have been transferred. The fibers are transferred from comb to comb in this manner until they have been sufficiently prepared.

9

Drawing off fibers
When the combing has been completed, the fibers are drawn off the comb. They can be drawn off in sections by holding one comb and grasping a section of fiber and pulling gently. These sections can then be spun. But, drawing off a long strand, called a top, is more desirable. To draw off a top, place the comb on a pad designed to hold the comb. Lace a few fibers through the hole of a diz (small gauge with hole to size the top) and commence pulling the fibers through the diz, a short length at a time, working hand over hand, until all fibers have been removed from the comb. The top can be wound around the arm for a continuous fiber supply while spinning.

111

10

Z and S twist
'Z' is clockwise twist
for singles. 'S' is
counterclockwise
for plying.

11 a

Attaching leader
Using spun yarn for a leader is simpler than spinning a leader, and it assists in locating the center of the cone when plying. A loop of yarn, tied at the end, can be looped back through itself to secure it to the shaft, then drawn up over the edge of the whorl, catching into the notch, and wound onto the hook of the high whorl spindle.

11 b

Joining to leader
When ready to spin, the fibers can be folded through the loop end to join fibers for spinning.

12

Initiating the draw
By initiating the draw prior to rolling the spindle on the thigh, a short unspun section is created. This section will absorb the initial twist and give the rolling hand time to get into position to control the flow of twist into the yarn.

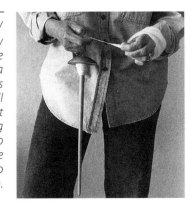

112

spun Lopi-type yarns). Because of the method of inserting the twist, this spindle is often referred to as a thigh or lap spindle. I am very partial to the high whorl hand spindle, both for the ease of control in spinning (appreciated by the beginner) and for its versatility (appreciated by the skilled).

10

Spindle spinning is an intermittent activity. First, twist is inserted while drawing out the fibers to create the yarn. Then the yarn is wound onto the spindle for storage. This is true for all spindle spinning. And, when spinning, if the spindle turns clockwise, 'Z' twist is inserted; if the spindle turns counterclockwise, 'S' twist is inserted. Traditionally, most singles are spun 'Z' while ply twist is 'S'. And, since we are thinking in terms of socks, it's good to know that many ethnic socks from this region do not require plied yarns. Many are knit of singles, others of two strands of singles worked as one but not plied. This does not mean that plying is difficult, only that not plying saves time.

Using the high whorl spindle suspended requires rolling the shaft on the thigh to set the spindle into motion. Many think that using a suspended spindle requires standing. Not necessarily; if seated, shorter lengths are spun prior to winding on.

As stated, the spindle is rolled on the thigh. It can be rolled down and away or up and toward the body. There are superstitions and old

wives' tales about the direction one must use, but I think that what is comfortable is what is best. Each spinner should find the way that feels 'right' and use it. If the spindle is rolled up and toward the body, 'Z' twist is inserted on the right side, 'S' twist on the left. Conversely, when rolling down and away, 'Z' twist is inserted on the left side, 'S' twist on the right.

Either hand can be used to hold the fiber supply and draw out the fibers. If the fiber supply is in the right hand, roll the spindle down and away from the body on the left. When the left hand holds the fibers, the right hand rolls the spindle up and toward the body on the right side.

11

To begin spinning, I attach a *leader* to the spindle. I use 24" to 30" of yarn, tying the ends together with an overhand knot in a long loop to attach to the spindle with a hitch at the knot end. The leader goes up and over the edge of the whorl to the hook. To spin clockwise, wind around the hook clockwise. Some high whorl spindles have a strategically placed notch or notches at the base that serve as a catch to lightly secure the yarn as it passes over the edge of the whorl to the hook. Catch the yarn into the notch and lay it across the top of the whorl to the right of the hook. Holding the yarn in this position, the spindle is turned clockwise one full turn to wind it into the hook.

When learning, use only a small fiber supply in the hand,

thus avoiding the danger that the 'tail' of the fiber supply will catch into the emerging yarn. With experience, a roving (long strand of lightly twisted, unspun fibers) can be wrapped around the wrist for a more continuous supply. To attach the fibers to the leader, lay a few fibers through the loop and start rolling the spindle to insert twist.

12 Initiate the draw prior to rolling the spindle so there will be a small unspun section to absorb the initial twist. This will keep the twist from advancing into the fiber supply. If twist gets into the fiber supply, the spindle will stop its rotation and promptly reverse itself. By initiating the draw prior to rolling the spindle, there is time to get this same hand into position to control the advancing twist. This sounds complicated to the novice, but it proves to be simple with just a little experimentation.

13 The suspended spindle lends itself to worsted spinning naturally. As the fibers are drawn from the supply, they begin to align themselves. The hand controlling the twist can also smooth the yarn. This enhances sheen and increases density — both characteristics of worsted yarns. Control of the spinning process is more easily achieved if both hands are in a level plane (hands held side by side, horizontally rather than vertically, one above the other). The newly

spun yarn travels over the curved fingers to the spindle. Thus, thumb and forefinger can readily control the advancing twist, keeping it from entering the fiber supply until drafting is complete.

14 Once a comfortable length of yarn is spun, it is ready to be wound onto the shaft of the spindle for storage. The newly spun yarn should be kept under tension so crook the index finger under the yarn, thus wrapping it around the finger and securing it. Grasp the bottom of the spindle and swing top (whorl) away from the body. By swinging the top away, the yarn in the hook moves to the bottom of the hook so that a quick counterclockwise revolution releases the yarn from the hook. With the yarn freed from the hook, it is wound onto the shaft clockwise.

15 This process is repeated, again and again, until a sizable cone of yarn is stored on the spindle. When winding on, the yarn should be wrapped firmly in a cone shape to maintain the balance. This is achieved by zigzagging up and down the shaft while winding on, always building further down the spindle. Or, the yarn can be wound on side by side to create the beehive shape preferred in the Middle East.

With a little bit of spinning experience, the high whorl spindle is very relaxing and the yarn builds rapidly. In no time at all, there will be enough yarn to knit a pair of

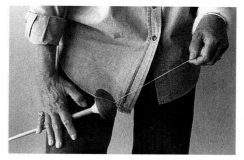

13

Spinning the yarn
With the spindle spinning, fibers are drawn out of the prepared wool evenly, the twist advancing into the drawn fibers to hold them together in the yarn.

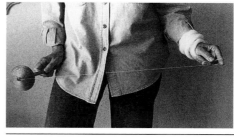

14

Releasing yarn from hook
When a length of yarn has been spun, it is ready to be stored on the shaft of the spindle. Yarn should be looped around end of finger to hold under tension. To release the yarn from the hook, grasp shaft at end and swing whorl away from body and turn spindle one revolution (counterclockwise for singles, clockwise for plying).

15

Storing yarn on spindle
Store yarn on the spindle while more is spun. Rotate the spindle in the same direction, and wind yarn onto the shaft in a zigzag motion.

113

Plying yarn
Yarn is plied from singles held on wooden knitting needles.

socks or stockings, for it requires only 8-10 ounces (400-600 yards) of a medium weight yarn for a pair of plain socks, 16-20 ounces (800-1200 yards) for elaborate color stranded patterned socks.

16 If the yarn is to be used as singles, skein the yarn and proceed to the finish bath or dye bath, as the case may be. Or, ply the yarn. There are several ways to approach plying. Many roll the yarn into a ball. I prefer to slip the cones off the spindle, storing them on a set of old wooden knitting needles until plying time. When ready to ply, I can slip two cones from the needles into my right hand or ply directly off the needles. By pulling up the leader (easily located if a colored yarn has been used), the beginning of the singles emerges so that the cones will serve as center pull balls. Keeping the two singles separated with my fingers, each is looped through the leader on the spindle and the spinning process repeated, this time spinning in the opposite direction for 'S' twist. For me, that means controlling the singles with my right hand.

Other fibers

Wool is not the only fiber used in Eastern ethnic socks and stockings. Occasionally, mohair from the Angora goat is used. Cotton is also popular throughout the area. In parts of Eastern Europe and Egypt, with the agricultural population necessary for cotton production, cotton socks were common. Farther east, the nomadic populations used wool from their flocks, trading for cotton when a true white yarn was desired. As was true in the weaving of the region, the brilliant white of cotton yarns was incorporated into the structure with the wool yarns that were readily dyed in glowing colors. Since cotton fibers are very short and fine in comparison to wool, the cotton yarns were always plied, most often 2-ply.

Selecting commercial yarns

For those seeking authenticity, this is a problem. When knitting Eastern ethnic socks and stockings, there is no commercial substitute for handspun yarn. It provides a vitality that no commercially spun yarn can equal. But, realistically, not everyone is going to spin his/her own yarn. A sport weight yarn is suitable for most of the socks and stockings under consideration (a fingering weight yarn for the finer gauges). As stated earlier, many of the yarns are used as singles, others as two strands of singles worked together but not plied, the remainder are 2-ply yarns. To be comparable, a fairly dense, worsted type yarn is necessary. The more primitive in appearance, the better it will serve the purpose.

We'll end where both the spinner-knitter and the non-spinning knitter begin
— with the yarn — skeins, balls, niddy-noddies and spindles full of yarn. Whether your choice extends
to the unspun fiber or begins with already-spun yarn, choose sturdy and knit firmly for ethnic socks and stockings.

Patterns & Abbreviations

Patterns

3 FOR P. 22, BAKHTIARI STOCKINGS.

Lower traveling stitch band. Multiple of 20 stitches **Rnd 1.** 1/1LC, k16, 1/1RC. **2.** K1, 1/1LC, k14, 1/1RC, k1. **3.** K2, 1/1LC, k12, 1/1RC, k2. **4.** K3, 1/1LC, k10, 1/1RC, k3. **5.** K4, 1/1LC, k8, 1/1RC, k4. **6.** K5, 1/1LC, k6, 1/1RC, k5. **7.** K6, 1/1LC, k4, 1/1RC, k6. **8.** K7, 1/1LC, k2, 1/1RC, k7. **9.** K8, 1/1LC, 1/1RC, k8. **10.** K9, 1/1RC, k9. **11-19.** Work Rows 9-1, reversing order of left and right crosses. **Upper traveling stitch band.** Multiple of 20 stitches **Rnd 1.** K4, 1/1LC, k14. **2.** K2, p2, k1, 1/1LC, k9, p2, k2. **3.** K6, 1/1LC, k12. **4.** K2, p2, k3, 1/1LC, k7, p2, k2. **5.** K8, 1/1LC, k10. **6.** K2, p2, k5, 1/1LC, k5, p2, k2. **7.** K10, 1/1LC, k8. **8.** K2, p2, k7, 1/1LC, k3, p2, k2. **9.** K12, 1/1LC, k6. **10.** K2, p2, k9, 1/1LC, k1, p2, k2. **11.** K14, 1/1LC, k4. Repeat Rnds 1-11. For methods to work 1/1LC *(knit over knit, left)* and 1/1RC *(knit over knit, right)* see pages 87 and 88.

4 FOR P. 24, LUR SOCKS.

Side panel. 6 stitches **Rnd 1.** P2, k2, p2. **2.** Knit. Repeat Rnds 1 and 2. **Diagonal pattern.** Multiple of 7 stitches. **Rnds 1, 3.** Purl. **2, 4.** Knit. **5.** K5, p2. **6.** K4, p2, k1. **7.** K3, p2, k2. **8.** K2, p2, k3. **9.** K1, p2, k4. **10.** P2, k5. **11.** P1, k5, p1. **12-23.** Repeat Rnds 5-11 and 5-9. **24.** Knit. **25-28.** Repeat Rnds 1-4.

8 FOR P. 31, NATURAL TURKISH STOCKINGS.

Traveling stitch rib. Multiple of 7 stitches **Rnd 1.** K1b, 1/1LC, 1/1RC, k1b, p1b. **2.** K1b, k1, 1/1LC, k1, k1b, p1b. **3.** K1b, 1/1RC, 1/1LC, k1b, p1b. **4.** K1b, k4, k1b, p1b. Repeat Rows 1-4. **Border pattern.** Multiple of 2 stitches **Rnds 1, 3.** Purl. **2.** Yo, k2tog.

18 FOR P. 48, FOOTED SOCKS FROM MACEDONIA.

Cable pattern. Multiple of 13 stitches **Rnds 1, 3, 5.** K1, yo, sl2tog-k1-p2sso, yo, k2, p1, k4, p1, k1. **2, 6.** K6, p1, k4, p1, k1. **4.** K6, p1; slip next 2 stitches to cable needle to front, k2, k2 from cable needle (2/2LC); p1, k1. Repeat Rnds 1-6.

19 FOR P. 51, BULGARIAN POINT PATTERN SOCK.

Lace panel. Over 5 stitches **Rnd 1.** P1, yo, sl2-k1-p2sso, yo, p1. **2-4.** P1, k3, p1. Repeat Rnds 1-4; end with Rnd 2.

6 FOR P. 97, BAKHTIARI SAMPLER. **Traveling stitch band.** Multiple of 8 sts. **Rnd 1.** K3, 1/1RC, k3. **2.** K2, 1/1RC, 1/1LC, k2. **3.** K1, 1/1RC, k2, 1/1LC, k1. **4.** 1/1RC, k4, 1/1LC. **5.** Slip first stitch of rnd, *k6, 1/1RC; rep from*, end 1/1RC with last st and first st of rnd. **6.** 1/1LC, k4, 1/1RC. **7.** K1, 1/1LC, k2, 1/1RC, k1. **8.** K2, 1/1LC, 1/1RC, k2. **9.** Same as Rnd 1.

Abbreviations

BO bind off

CO cast on

dec decrease

inc increase

k knit

k1b knit in back of loop to twist stitch (for Western stitch mount)

k2tog knit 2 together

p purl

p1b purl in back of loop to twist stitch (for Western stitch mount)

p2tog purl 2 together

rep repeat

rnd round

sl2tog-k1-p2sso slip 2 stitches together, knit 1, pass 2 slipped stitches over

SSK slip, slip, knit

st stitch

twisted knit knit in the back loop (unless stitch is mounted in the Eastern fashion)

twisted purl purl in the back loop (unless stitch is mounted in the Eastern fashion)

1/2 rib Generally the first number applies to the knits, the second to the purls.

Let us give cheers for that age when again many beautiful
unsigned goods are produced . . . the time when again such beautiful goods
are used as a matter of course in daily life. THE UNKNOWN CRAFTSMAN *by Soetsu Yanagi, 1972*

References

1 de Dillmont, Therese. THE COMPLETE ENCYCLOPEDIA OF NEEDLEWORK, Philadelphia, PA: Running Press, 1978 (originally published in 1886).

2 Eek, Ann Christine. 'Folkelig Albansk Kulture,' *Norsk Husflid #2*, Oslo, Norway: Norges Husflidslag, 1993.

3 Gibson-Roberts, Priscilla A. 'Bulgarian Stockings — Motif Knitting,' *Piecework Vol. II, #4*, Loveland, CO: Interweave Press, Inc., 1994.

4 Gibson-Roberts, Priscilla A. 'His Gloves from Iran,' *Knitter's Magazine #33*, Sioux Falls, SD: XRX, Inc., 1993.

5 Gibson-Roberts, Priscilla A. 'Summer Spinning, A Return to the Hand Spindle,' part 1, and 'Handspun Yarns for Ethnic Socks,' part 2, *Knitter's Magazine #35* and *#36*, Sioux Falls, SD: XRX, Inc., 1994.

6 Gibson-Roberts, Priscilla A. 'Ukrainian Stockings,' *Knitter's Magazine, #28*, Sioux Falls, SD: XRX, Inc., 1992.

7 Harrell, Betsy. ANATOLIAN KNITTING DESIGNS: SIVAS STOCKING PATTERNS COLLECTED IN AN ISTANBUL SHANTYTOWN, Istanbul, Turkey: Redhouse Press, 1981.

8 Ioannou-Yanara, Tatiana. THE GREEK FOLK COSTUME: COSTUMES OF THE SIGOUNI, Athens, Greece: Melissa Publishing House, 1977.

Macvnhkob, Vobeh. COONNCKA BE3BA, Bulgaria: Coonr, 1973

9 Ozbel, Kenan. KNITTED STOCKINGS FROM TURKISH VILLAGES, Istanbul, Turkey: Cultural Publications, 1981.

10 Raven, Lee. HANDS ON SPINNING, Loveland, CO: Interweave Press, 1987.

11 Saliklis, Ruta. A WEALTH OF PATTERN: NORTHERN EUROPEAN AND MIDDLE EASTERN FOLK KNITTING IN THE HELEN ALLEN TEXTILE COLLECTION, Madison: University of Wisconsin, 1990.

12 Thomas, Mary. MARY THOMAS'S KNITTING BOOK, New York: Dover Publications, Inc., 1972.

13 Thurner, Noel. 'Viking Wool Combs,' *Spin-off, Vol. XVI, #1*, Loveland, CO: Interweave Press, Inc., 1992.

14 Zilboorg, Anna. FANCY FEET: TRADITIONAL KNITTING PATTERNS OF TURKEY, Asheville, NC: Altamont Press, 1994.

15 Zilboorg, Anna. 'The Rich Tradition of Turkish Knitted Stockings,' *Piecework, Vol. I, #2*, Loveland, CO: Interweave Press, Inc: 1993.

This book represents the first phase of an ongoing study of Eastern ethnic socks.
Anyone with relevant information, especially socks to be documented and recorded,
is requested to contact the author through XRX, Inc., PO Box 1525, Sioux Falls, SD 57101-1525.

Index

119

Colophon

This book, written by a knitter and produced by knitters, was printed on matte paper using the following fonts: for the large sock identification numbers, *Papyrus* by Letraset, a typeface evocative of the East and Egypt, the land where the earliest piece of knitting has been found. For readability, the text was set in Adobe *Goudy*, a classic typeface. Because of the multiple demands placed on the display type (headlines; photo, illustration, and chart captions), Adobe *Myriad* was used, a font that allows text to be 'elastically' fitted into a space. (It made for such a beautiful 'fit,' you'd think it was designed with knitters in mind.)

Using Apple Macintosh™ and Power Macintosh™ computers, the page make-up program *QuarkXPress*™ allowed precision typesetting and integration of text with illustrations and photographic images. The program of choice for making high-quality color and black-and-white charts and symbols was Adobe *Illustrator.*™ Adobe *Photoshop*™ made possible the presentation of photo-captured images with precision and gave us the ability to do the necessary enhancements making the photographs easier to understand and to print.

This image manipulation, under the guidance of digital consultant David Xenakis, sometimes took amusing turns. Take the Turkish cabled sock that wraps the book's cover. The actual sock, knit in the round, contained too few repeats to span the distance. And we knew Priscilla A. Gibson-Roberts wouldn't hear of cutting this precious sock so that it could be folded out and photographed, even though we promised it would be invisibly grafted together afterwards by the finest on the staff of *Knitter's Magazine*… So there was only one thing to do: let David do the cutting and grafting — on his computer screen!

Photographer Alexis Xenakis used medium and view cameras (Hasselblad 201F and Sinar 4X5) to insure clear, sharp images. Now, you too can count every stitch — just as Priscilla did!